Nana,

Thank you for always inspiring me to grow.
I'm forever grateful for your unconditional
love and consistent support.

BECOME A BETTER Y🌍U ABROAD

Ditch Your Comfort Zone for Self Growth
Through the 10 Skills You'll Gain by Studying Abroad

SAMANTHA KAISER

Cover design by 100Covers.com
Formatted by FormattedBooks.com

ISBN: 978-1-7348084-0-7 (Paperback)
ISBN: 978-1-7348084-1-4 (mobi)
ISBN: 978-1-7348084-2-1 (ePub)

DOWNLOAD THE WORK BOOK FREE!

Just to say thanks for buying my book, I would like to give you a work book to help guide you through the beginning phase of studying abroad!

I know how overwhelming the beginning process of applying was for me, so I've included helpful tools to make it easier for you!

TO DOWNLOAD GO TO:

https://www.subscribepage.com/studyabroadworkbook

CONTENTS

INTRODUCTION

Have you considered studying abroad but it doesn't seem like the right time? Does the beginning process seem overwhelming, tedious, and time consuming? Studying abroad is a commitment, but one that will give you lifelong skills! Through the process, you'll gain global awareness and grow as an individual.

As a study abroad alumnus, I've reaped the benefits that studying abroad has provided me. I studied abroad in Salamanca, Spain for two months over the summer of 2018. I experienced self-growth and gained skills that have benefited me ever since. I had such a positive experience that I want to encourage others to step out of their comfort zone!

Maybe you've already decided on going abroad, and you've done all the hard work to go. Now, you're excited and ready to take on the challenge ahead. If you want to make the most out of your study abroad experience by reflecting, this is a perfect book for you. I explain step-by-step which skills you gain before you go, during your trip, and after your arrival back home.

I divide this book into three sections: skills acquired before, during, and after your trip. These skills include: openness to experience, bravery, mindfulness, adaptability, empathy, wisdom, authenticity, gratitude, resilience, and leadership. If you have any interest in strengthening these skills abroad, you're in the right place!

In this book, you'll find the motivation to step out of your comfort zone. This book encourages you to become a better you, using the skills you learn abroad. I describe the positive transformation I underwent abroad through meaningful, personal stories. Studying abroad led me to personal growth and opportunities I never knew existed.

One of my favorite memories of studying abroad was the Running of the Bulls festival in Pamplona. If you don't know what this festival is, don't fret, I'll give a brief description in the next section! The emotions I felt throughout the run closely resembled the emotions I felt abroad! I use the Running of the Bulls as a metaphor to identify the emotions I felt during each phase of the experience.

Studying abroad can seem scary and overwhelming, but anything that involves growth does. After you've read this book, I promise that you'll understand the benefits of studying abroad. It can supply you with lifelong assets and grant you leadership opportunities. If you're still unsure about studying abroad, this is the perfect book to guide you in the right direction. Don't let this magnificent opportunity pass you by!

I'm here to be your emotional support, guide, and friend along the way! I know you have what it takes to make the leap abroad! You too have the potential for an eye-opening, transformative experience!

RUNNING OF THE BULLS

A BRIEF DESCRIPTION

Every July, thousands of people gather to celebrate the San Fermin festival, which is over a week long and takes place in Pamplona, Spain. The festival dates back to the early 1500s, honoring Saint Fermin, the patron Saint of the Navarra region.

The festival starts on the afternoon of July 6th and ends midnight July 14th. One of the most famous events of the festival is the running of the bulls.

Yes, it's exactly what it sounds like. Twelve bulls are set free from a corral as thousands of daredevils crowd the streets. Once the bulls are released, the participants run with the thousand-pound bulls for a half mile. The race ends in a bullfighting arena. Wooden fences and posts block off side streets to maintain a workable course.

The run begins at 8am on July 7th and continues each morning until the 14th. Each participant is required to wear white pants, a white shirt, and a red scarf around their waist. The bulls are chosen based on of their size, color, and breed.

At 8am sharp, an official fires a starting pistol, indicating the release of six bulls. These are the six bulls that are used in the post-run bullfighting. Once these six bulls have entered the arena, another shot is fired. Then, another six bulls enter the streets. Once all twelve bulls have entered the arena, the last shot is fired, indicating the run is over.

The run usually lasts about five minutes but can vary from two to six minutes if a bull is separated from the herd. In that case, it's the duty of experienced runners to guide the bull into the arena. Once the bulls enter the arena, they're guided to another corral on the opposite side of where they entered.

The gates to the bullfighting arena close once all twelve bulls have entered. Nobody can enter the arena after that. Running of the bulls dates back to the early fourteenth century and continues on to this day. Because of controversial debates about whether the run is ethical or not, authorities may call for termination of the run in the future.

DISCLAIMER: I decided to travel to Pamplona and attend the festival on my own time. It wasn't part of the study abroad program excursions. Academic Programs International does not encourage dangerous behavior, and I participated in the run at my own risk.

Some names have been changed in this book to maintain privacy.

LIFE BEFORE YOU LEAVE

Waiting for the Starting Pistol

A s I paced down the narrow streets of Pamplona, my eyes were drawn to the bright red and green flags. They hung from apartment balconies and wooden fences. I heard nervous chatter around me, as business owners boarded up their doors and windows. They were blocking themselves from the crowded street. Chaos would soon be taking place.

Along the roads, beer cans, wrappers, and water bottles covered the gutters. Obviously, plenty of partying had been going on the night before. Some people in the crowd smelled of Spanish beer, and it appeared that they hadn't even gone to bed. They had giddy, drunken smiles and dark purple bags underneath glazed eyes. The weeklong festival called for celebration, and everybody seemed to be worry free.

Everybody wore white pants and shirts, with red scarves around their waists. Some people wore red bandannas on their necks, too. I was one of them. Even at 7:30 in the morning, the city was alive. A swarm of people huddled around the wooden gates, trying to mark their spot. Everybody wanted to watch the annual San Fermin Running with the Bulls run.

My childhood best friend Cassie was visiting me from Minnesota. Both of our parents enrolled us into a Spanish immersion program. Throughout elementary school, we had learned about the Running of the Bulls festival. It was hard to believe we were walking through the streets of Pamplona in real life. Both of us were adrenaline junkies to say the least, so we had always wanted to participate. It was incredible that ten years later, we had actually made it happen.

Beforehand, an experienced runner gave us some advice for the run. She advised us that if we wanted to make it into the arena, we should start our run after a street named "Encierro." It was the first sharp turn in the race, and she advised us to stand on the right side of the street. The turn was too sharp for the thousand-pound animals to clear. Thus, the bulls would slam into wooden gates that blocked off the course on the left side.

When Cassie and I heard this, we exchanged a quick glance at each other and nervously giggled. Sure, we had learned about this in elementary school. But as we strolled down those streets, the realness of it all sunk in. We walked in silent unison, taking it all in.

After a couple of minutes of walking, we reached the corner with a sign on the building reading "Encierro." We settled near the wall on the right side near the corner among the crowd of people. Glancing down at my watch, I saw it was 7:45. "Fifteen minutes!" I squealed, squeezing my best friend's hand.

Our nervousness and excitement made us jittery and hyper-active. It was lightly drizzling, which made me a bit concerned that the streets would be slippery. It also didn't help that I was going to be running with a sprained ankle. Fortunately, the rain never escalated from a mist, and the weather was tolerable. The chilly morning air was crisp against my skin but felt refreshing.

All of a sudden, I heard raised voices, and people started bumping into me, trying to move forward. I shot a glance behind me and was utterly confused. Five Spanish police were walking in a line across the street, heading toward the runners.

They walked slowly, pushing the crowd forward. There was no way to get through them. Everybody around me was looking for answers, but nobody seemed to know what was going on. We inched our way forward, hoping the police would eventually stop walking.

They didn't, and they ushered us off to a side street and off the course entirely. My best friend and I looked at each other frantically with fear in our eyes. We made the commitment to risk our lives to participate in this once-in-a-lifetime run. Yet, the opportunity was slipping from our fingertips.

"What do we do?" I whined, feeling panic.

"There's got to be a way in," she voiced determinedly. She grabbed my hand, and off we went, searching for a way back into the race.

We only had ten minutes until the race. We were sprinting through alleyways, trying to find an opening to the course. Police stood at every gate, and the chance of reentering didn't seem promising. We stopped at one entry, and police held out their hand, signaling we couldn't enter. We scurried to a different opening with the same results.

Feeling flustered, we hurried up the street toward another entry. I told the bystanders standing at the wooden fences that I wanted to enter the race. Two people understandingly stepped aside for me to enter. I huddled down, swung my leg over a board, and then stepped into the street. As soon as I stood up, my eyes landed on policemen in front of me.

I felt fear wash over me once again, afraid police would usher me off the street for the second time. The police ushered me into the street, allowing me to enter. *Finally, I'm in,* I thought as I let out a big sigh of relief. I looked behind me, but I couldn't find Cassie anywhere.

"Sam!" I heard her yell from the other side of the fence. "Cassie!" I screamed back. I waddled my way back to the fence where I saw my best friend on the other side. "Come through here, they'll let you in!" I motioned, grabbing her hand and pulling her through. As soon as she made it to the other side, we both relaxed a little bit. That didn't last long, though. We realized the fence we had crossed led us to the beginning of the race.

We strutted to the nearest opening on the side of the street, contemplating our next steps. The clock on her phone read 7:53. We debated staying at the front, considering how difficult it was to even enter the race. A bystander overheard our conversation and said with a serious face, "This is the most dangerous part of the run." Cassie and I exchanged looks and stood for a moment in silence.

I examined my surroundings, and a different kind of fear entered my nervous system. You know the feeling where your body falls cold and your stomach drops to the floor? Yeah, it was that kind of fear. As I looked at the people around us, one thing stood out in common; they were all male.

My voice began to waver as I pointed this out to my best friend. "We're the only females here," I gulped. "Let's try to make it back to the corner so we can make it into the arena?" I asked hoping she would agree. She grabbed my hand and nodded, glancing back down at her clock. 7:56. We had four minutes to get there.

In four minutes, six bulls would be set loose onto the enclosed streets of Pamplona. Thousands of people would be sprinting alongside the bulls, running toward the arena. Could we make it to the corner in four minutes? We sprinted through the crowded streets, pulling our weight as fast as we could.

My adrenaline was pumping so hard I couldn't even feel the pain in my sprained ankle. We pushed and pushed for what felt like an eternity. Finally, we saw the corner up ahead. I felt a hint of reassurance, and as we turned the corner and eased our pace, I finally had time to catch my breath.

We returned to where we were standing before the police pushed us off the course, then we checked the time. 7:57. I looked around and felt comfort when I saw females standing nearby. It's hard to feel comfort, though, when you only have three minutes before the madness begins. My heart started beating intensely. It felt like a million butterflies had flown into my stomach. I was the perfect mix of excited and nervous.

I started to feel balls of sweat gather on my forehead and the palm of my hands. I looked down, and I realized I was still clenching Cassie's hand. "Don't let go, okay?" I stated intensely, giving it a squeeze. "Never," she reassured me. "One minute to go. Are you ready?" she asked, giving a little jump of excitement. "More ready now than ever," I replied, feeling a flutter of exhilaration in my heart.

OPENNESS TO EXPERIENCE

"Let go of certainty. The opposite isn't uncertainty. It's openness, curiosity and a willingness to embrace paradox, rather than choose up sides. The ultimate challenge is to accept ourselves exactly as we are, but never stop trying to learn and grow." —Tony Schwartz

"The doors will be opened to those who are bold enough to knock." —Unknown

Have you ever had a goal you wanted to accomplish in the future, but the future arrives, and it seems like the wrong time? Maybe you had a class project due for months but procrastinated until a few days before the deadline. Maybe you wanted to take a vacation over spring break, but disregarded saving up for it.

Odds are, we've all had a goal we've wanted to fulfill in our lives that we end up blowing off because we blame it on bad timing. At first, that was what the first steps to studying abroad felt like for me. Being bilingual, I had always known I wanted to study abroad. Nevertheless, when my sophomore year of college ended, the timing didn't feel *right*.

Maybe you're like me and knew you wanted to study abroad. Yet, when it's time to start planning, you feel unprepared and that the time passed by too quickly. Maybe the idea of studying abroad has entered your head but it seems overwhelming.

The first thing that I learned from my study abroad experience is that the perfect time is now. No major life-changing decision feels like the right time! Life can be busy, schedules can be crammed, but life doesn't stop for anybody. I had dreamed of Running with the Bulls since I was a fearless ten-year-old. It *definitely* wasn't the perfect timing to run with a sprained ankle. But I knew that opportunity would never arise again.

It's easy to take the safe and comfortable way out of achieving the goals you set for yourself. It's easy to let them pass you by. Sometimes, we feel like we're open to trying new things; however, our excuses get in the way of achieving this. Studying abroad taught me that seizing opportunities leads you to helpful learning possibilities. It also taught me that being open to new experiences helps build your self-awareness. It may seem like it isn't the perfect time, but it's time to act now! Studying abroad is a limited opportunity that's only offered through educational institutions.

If you blame timing on the goals or dreams that you want to accomplish, they'll always stay ideas. Thinking about your goal can fill you with excitement and drive! Still, pushing yourself out of your comfort zone to obtain that goal can be uncomfortable. That's exactly what openness to experience feels like.

Openness to experience is a messy mixture of pure excitement and willingness to embrace the discomfort. Beginning to accomplish a goal, habit, or challenge is always the hardest part.

Nonetheless, if you're even *considering* studying abroad, I have great news for you! You're open to new experiences! If you're willing to seize this window of opportunity, you'll accumulate useful life skills. You'll also have intriguing stories to tell afterwards!

I was uncomfortable leaving my home country at first. Once I overcame that, I was naturally open to new experiences. Once you're willing to try new things, engaging experiences become limitless. Once you begin stepping out of your comfort zone, it becomes easier each time.

For the most part, I'm not a picky eater. So, when I arrived in Spain, I wasn't worried about trying the food. Despite that, I felt my stomach twist when I walked into my host family's kitchen the first day. On the counter, I saw pork sitting out on a plate right next to the fridge.

Finding out Spaniards sometimes leave pork out a few hours before eating made me feel uneasy, to say the least. I seriously felt my appetite hop on a bus to France. They also kept milk outside of the refrigerator, too!

In the United States, I'm used to seeing warning labels scream at me to refrigerate items immediately after opening. In middle school, a teen chef teacher wired this into my brain. She warned my class that meat harvests bacteria in under two hours after sitting out. The seriousness of her voice is forever sketched into my brain. I could feel my mind flip through all the worst-case scenarios. My mind screamed at me I would become sick if I ate or drank anything left out.

It wasn't just my host family who kept meat sitting out. Meat shops and restaurants around town would have meat hanging as a display in the windows! That was when I realized that being open to trying new things wasn't a skill you could master right away...

it was something you could practice every day by adjusting your mindset! An open mind allows you to try new things and reveals how there's always a different way to look at things.

Feeling uneasy about the pork and milk situation, I casually brought it up to my host dad, Jorge. I hoped my facial expression didn't display obvious disgust. Jorge explained that Spain processes meat and dairy products differently than the United States does. Spain's meat industry has high-quality-controlled food safety regulations. He promised it was completely safe to eat. They actually leave it out for a few hours to give the pork a rich flavor.

They pasteurize milk differently in Europe than they do the United States. The difference is that milk stays good for months outside of the fridge. On the other hand, in the United States, milk stays good for a couple of weeks inside of the refrigerator. Eating pork that sat out was a little nerve racking that first meal. Drinking room temperature milk also took some getting used to. Nonetheless, it taught me that there's never one way of doing things.

As soon as I conquered the pork and milk situation, I decided to take my taste buds to the next level. Remember when I mentioned restaurants with meat hanging as a display in the window? Yeah, that next level.

In Spain, you could find one of these restaurants titled "Doner Kebabs" on every corner. Kebabs originated in Turkey, and they're somewhat like a Gyro in America. Walking into a Kebab restaurant for the first time was unappealing to me. Three different kinds of meat slowly rotated from spears that hung from the ceiling. Even though I had opened up my mind to trying different foods, it still made me uneasy.

I slowly stepped foot into a restaurant that had red and black checkered floors and took my place in line. The person in the front of the line ordered, and as he stepped away from the register, I became even more uneasy. The man behind the counter took a knife and shaved off thin strips of meat into a paper bowl!

I realized I was biting my nails and bouncing one of my legs. Those were both unhealthy habits I engage in while dealing with my anxiety. I inched forward, squinting at the menu above the counter. I decided to get a Kebab with lamb and roasted vegetables. I took a deep breath and stepped up to the counter. I completed my order with a shaky voice, diving right into uncomfortability.

As soon as I paid, I sat down in the nearest booth trying to calm myself down. I watched people walking past the restaurant to distract my mind. A couple minutes passed, and finally the worker plopped down my Kebab on the table right in front of me. A thick breaded tortilla held onions, tomatoes, lamb, and zucchini in a perfect taco shape. I had to admit, it did look delicious.

I held my breath as I brought the Kebab up to my mouth. I closed my eyes, opened my mouth, and as I took my first bite, a satisfactory groan left my mouth. The groan surprised me. "Mmm," I groaned while chewing. I sunk into the booth, intrigued by the rich flavor that entered my mouth.

The vegetables were perfectly grilled. The meat was so savory my mouth watered between bites! I topped it off with sauce blanche; a mayo-yogurt sauce that added the perfect touch. I had never tasted anything like it before. From then on, Kebab was my absolute favorite meal and still is to this day.

I felt disgusted with myself for ever being skeptical. Still, this experience encouraged me to open my mind to a variety of things, moving forward. I bought at least ten Kebabs while I studied abroad, and, even today, a Gyro doesn't come close in comparison. By being open and pushing through my skepticism, I tasted one of the most scrumptious foods ever.

If studying abroad has even entered your mind, you're already one step ahead. You're willing to try new things with an open mind! It's important not to let timing or fear steer you away from the amazing experience you could endure ahead.

People who are open generally tend to be intellectually curious with active imaginations. They're also usually more emotionally intelligent. Being open can create opportunities to develop new relationships in your life. When you're willing to try new things, you're more likely to acquire more experiences than those who aren't. This usually leads to having plenty of adventurous stories to tell!

Living a life that's comfortable is okay. Nevertheless, opening yourself up to new experiences leads to growth of knowledge. It also allows you to see different perspectives. It's fantastic that you're thinking about studying abroad! This means you're willing to step out of your comfort zone into new perspectives and experiences. This can only enrich your life.

I was extremely nervous and excited to run with the bulls. I felt the same way about eating left out meat and milk. In the end, being open to trying these things led me to the most defining memories. If you do decide to study abroad, I promise you your openness to experience will only grow stronger!

Don't let your goals, dreams, and aspirations continue to stay ideas. It's up to you to take the risk to live out your dreams, rather than living a stagnant life. I dare you to step out of your comfort zone and open yourself up to trying something new. Worst case scenario, you learn from the experience. You'll also have a better understanding of what your interests are. I encourage you to step into a life of growth, instead of stepping back into the life of safety.

BRAVERY

"You cannot swim for new horizons until you have courage to lose sight of the shore." —William Faulkner

"Always go with the choice that scares you the most, because that's the one that is going to help you grow." —Caroline Myss

"You gain strength, courage and confidence by every experience in which you really stop to look fear in the face. You must do the thing you think you cannot do." —Eleanor Roosevelt

Once you open your mind to the idea of studying abroad, you'll have to make plenty of decisions. It can feel overwhelming and confusing at first. You'll have to contemplate where you'll want to go and how long you'll want to stay. You'll have to decide which living arrangements you prefer and how to cover your expenses. You'll also need to think about which classes you'll want to take.

It's okay to feel overwhelmed because it's all part of the process. Trust the process, because you'll achieve skills that will benefit you forever. All the overwhelming emotions you're feeling are completely normal. Remember, nothing worthwhile comes easy!

Think of all the difficult decisions and all the tedious tasks you've had to do in your life. Think of them as hurdles in your route or police pushing you off the road. Once you clear the hurdle or make it back onto the course, you're one step closer to finishing the race!

Don't let these challenges discourage you. You're strong, courageous, and I'm 100% convinced you're ready to take on this opportunity. I remember packing for Spain and feeling completely overwhelmed. I had no idea what to pack! I had to leave in four days, and I was panicking. I had to take an hour break to reset my mind and remind myself to be brave.

Bravery is one of the most crucial skills to practice before you leave abroad. It's what drives you to take your first steps getting out of the car and into the airport. Once your bravery carries you through, you'll feel relieved that you didn't take the easy way out!

Being open to trying new things is one thing. Actually having the bravery to follow through is another. Leaving your comfort zone can feel extremely terrifying and overwhelming at first. I remember as my family dropped me off at the airport, I felt a lot of things all at once. I stood in line for security and thought to myself, *Wow. I'm going to a foreign country for two months where I won't know **anybody***.

I felt afraid of the uncertainty of what was to come next in my journey. Leaving what's comfortable for something that isn't can bring anxiety and fear. The key is to face your fears instead of running from them. (Unless you're in the path of bulls in Pamplona, of course. Then I would suggest running).

If we always took the safe way out, our lives would be stagnant. Nothing would ever change. We would all be living with the same knowledge, and we would all hear the same stories. Our lives would be devoid of personal and societal growth.

What if Rosa Parks didn't feel that urge to stand her ground when someone asked to take her seat? What if NASA never attempted to land on the moon? Lewis, Clark, and Sacagawea didn't discover new land by letting their fear convince them to stay home!

Many times, we brush off our courageousness because we're afraid to fail. Failure is scary, yes, but there's no way to succeed unless you're open to failure. When you combine openness to an unknown outcome with the bravery to try, nothing can hold you back!

Traveling to Europe was my first time solo traveling. I felt terrified being a continent away from everything I had ever known. Walking through the airport alone was intimidating. At the same time, it brought a warm and powerful feeling that washed over my body. I felt invincible. It was the first time I had acknowledged my own bravery.

Traveling to a different country alone gave me the bravery to travel alone in the future! Eventually, I was planning solo trips around Spain by choice! I had one weekend left before my program would end, and I wanted to try traveling on my own. I decided to book a day trip to Valladolid, about an hour and a half train ride from Salamanca.

I boarded the fast train all by myself at 8 in the morning and was on my way to a new adventure. I zoomed past open fields and dainty towns as my mind wandered to the possibilities ahead. This time around, I felt excited about the unknown, not afraid of it. The time passed, I swung my backpack onto my shoulders, and stepped off the train.

Once I set foot into the town, it was eerily quiet. I walked for about half a mile toward the main street and realized that it was still fairly early in the morning. Stores and museums wouldn't be open for a couple of hours! Luckily, there was a beautiful park right next to the train stop that I excitedly explored.

Stepping inside of the park felt like entering a completely different environment. The rich evergreen brush was so thick; greenery surrounded me. I was apart from the outside world. Pink roses enchanted the gravel path, and the birds were singing their morning songs.

I jumped a little when I looked ahead and saw a massive peacock spreading out its vibrant feathers in front of me. They were everywhere! I was so awestruck I held my hand over my mouth, refusing to let my giggles awake the silence of the crisp morning air. I admit, I was also a little scared to agitate the large birds.

As I strolled, I admired statues, ponds, and the rich scent of flowers in harmony. It was only the beginning of my adventure, but I was off to a great start, feeling at peace with the earth.

Once ten o'clock came around, I stopped at a tourist shop next to the park. I fetched a map of the city, since I didn't have data for a GPS. I sat on a nearby bench and made a route for myself, making stops at locations and museums I wanted to explore. I began my solo adventure, feeling fearless. I knew if I could travel to a different country all on my own, traveling to a city alone would be a walk in the park (pun intended).

I admired the gorgeous monumental architecture that surrounded me in Valladolid. Tall, cream-colored stone buildings encapsulated me with their detailed carvings. The carvings consisted of angels, gods, people, animals, and anything you could imagine. Even though the city was fairly close to Salamanca, it was completely unique in its own way.

I arrived at my first stop, the house where Miguel de Cervantes resided. Next, the cathedral. After, I stopped at the Valladolid museum, and then, I found myself at the Cristopher Columbus museum. That was when I realized I was out of euros and, unfortunately, they didn't accept credit cards. As I went museum to museum afterwards, I had the same results.

I felt a little bummed out, but I decided to change my course. At this point, I could have let the fear of uncertainty bring me down, but I decided to improvise. I made my way to the river and found a cute little authentic bar where they accepted credit cards. I had a couple of Spanish appetizers and a cocktail. I enjoyed the warmth on my skin with the sound of the river flowing in the background.

Once I was finished with my appetizers, I walked to a garden nearby. I paced the overgrown aisles of grass, brush, and flowers. I took it all in, amazed by the natural beauty. I noticed an art museum across the street and decided to give it a shot. After all, I had nothing to lose. When I stepped through the glass doors, I was pleased to find out the museum was free for students.

I explored the museum and realized the day had passed me by. I couldn't believe it was already time to make my way back to the train station to head back to Salamanca. I strolled back, feeling content.

All in all, I had a great time exploring a different city all on my own. I felt confident and brave and capable of achieving anything I put my mind to.

I discovered on my trip to Valladolid that even though you can plan ahead, some things don't work out. You can plan for what you want to do and see, but there will always be beauty in things you never saw coming. Sure, I had planned to navigate more museums. But I never planned on finding the cute bar on the river. I didn't plan on going to the free art museum or finding the peacock filled park next to the train station.

Before I left for this trip, I would never have had the courage to try something so subjective to change! Although I felt scared to travel alone, I endured bravery to get there. My bravery brought me self-confidence to travel by myself later on.

I could have planned more carefully and brought more euros with me. However, I was brave enough to try something new and be willing to fail in the process. With a little bravery and improvisation, I succeeded in traveling alone. Not only that, but I had a fantastic time doing it.

The bravery I endured on that trip brought me confidence and responsibility. Bravery allows you to be confident in who you are and the ability to disregard what other people think of you. The story I'm about to tell brings out a different benefit of bravery: feeling comfortable in your own skin.

One night, Cassie and I had ventured out to a popular club in Salamanca. The club always had fun events happening. They had a mechanical bull, beer pong tournaments, karaoke, you name it. Well, the night that Cassie and I had gone, they had a dance off challenge.

I have to admit, I was already a gin and tonic in, and Cassie wasn't completely sober, either. We heard the announcer inform the crowd where to sign up. Naturally, Cassie grabbed my hand and with daring eyes said, "Sam, we *have* to do it."

I was a little hesitant at first, but I'm easily convinced. I would consider this a blessing and a curse. Without knowing much about what we were getting into, we walked on stage and gave the announcer our names. He gave a quick smirk and wrote our names on a sheet of paper.

The next thing I knew, I heard the announcer dramatically call us up, "Saaaam and Cassieeeee to the stage please!" We made our way through the crowd and up the steps onto the small stage, not realizing what was about to happen.

We stood next to two other girls who were Spaniards and waited for instructions. I looked at the crowd and saw about fifty pairs of eyes looking back at me. I already had a fear of public speaking, so I had no idea how I was going to dance in front of all of these people.

As the announcer addressed the rules of the dance off, my stomach began to twist. We had to dance to a full Reggaeton song, and, at the end, whichever team had the loudest applause won. It seems easy enough, right?

The catch was that Reggaeton is a type of Spanish music that includes very sexual lyrics and dancing. Neither Cassie nor I were the best dancers to start off with. On that note, we *definitely* didn't know how to dance provocatively. I'm the type of girl who dances with her shoulders, not her hips. It didn't help that our competition was clearly from Spain and probably knew what they were doing.

It felt like a nightmare where you show up to class naked for a test. The only problem: I wasn't dreaming. The announcer started a countdown. Cassie took my hand and whispered to me "We got this" as I stared at the crowd with wide eyes. My mind was racing a thousand miles per hour, thinking of how I was going to pull this off.

The music began and a seductive woman's voice accompanied the melody. Cassie and I held hands facing each other, swaying our hips in each direction. I tried to dance on rhythm, but after about thirty seconds, I gave up trying to impress the audience. I decided to have fun with it.

I started twirling Cassie around and we shimmied close to each other. We weren't able to resist outbursts of laughter. It might've been embarrassing, but we were having a blast. We danced our hearts out as well as we could to the music. When the song ended and it was time to catch our breaths, we stood there with cheesy grins on our faces.

We faced the crowd for the first time after the music had stopped. When it was the crowd's turn to cheer for the winner, about three Americans cheered for us in the front. We burst out in full belly laughter and threw our fists in the air, as if we had won. My nervousness was gone.

The crowd erupted in applause for the girls standing next to us, but we weren't phased. We weren't there to win; we just wanted to have fun. It took a lot of bravery getting up onto that stage, but once we did, we were embracing ourselves. We decided to ignore what the rest of the world thought. That, my friend, is a magical feeling.

Daring to be brave can open up a world of possibilities for you. Bravery is an important lifelong skill. It enables you to challenge and push yourself to overcome the things that hold you back. Nonetheless, bravery encourages you to have fun. If Cassie hadn't encouraged me to step on that stage, I probably would've only been one of the people cheering in the audience.

When I first started my classes abroad, I felt terrified to attempt to speak Spanish in front of the class. I was afraid my classmates would judge me on my pronunciation and fluency. Once I had the nerve to speak up, it became easier every time, and my confidence grew in my abilities!

Being brave can be daunting; however, the more you practice it, the easier it will come. Do you think I woke up the morning of Running with the Bulls calm and collected? Absolutely not! I knew that it was dangerous, and I could get seriously injured! But what fun is it to sit on the sidelines and watch everybody else go through something incredibly fantastic? What fun is it to cheer from the audience when you could be the one dancing on stage?

I felt terrified that I would be one of the few females participating in the run. My bravery pushed me to endure a once-in-a-lifetime-experience. Facing your fears equips you with the bravery to overcome the challenges ahead.

It's fantastic that you're open to experience. I know you're brave enough to take that next step and create lasting memories abroad. You too can step onto the stage. You too, can be a runner.

THE JOURNEY ABROAD

The Run

*B*OOM, thundered the starting pistol. In an instant, my heartbeat accelerated and my stomach dropped. All of my senses intensified. I was so awake, I felt like I had downed five cups of coffee. I intently watched behind me, observing the motions of those surrounding me.

After a minute that seemed like ten seconds, I felt the ground trembling. I couldn't wrap my mind around the fact that I could actually feel the stomping of the bulls' hooves. I started to become alarmingly aware of the feeling in my legs.

After a couple of seconds, the runners around us started jogging. Cassie and I followed their lead. We intertwined our fingers, holding hands with a tight grip, so that we wouldn't get separated. The woman who had given us advice before the run had warned us that we would get separated from each other. We were eager to prove her wrong, and we promised to hold on as tightly as we could.

We had been jogging for a couple strides with the crowd when I heard a new sound. Cow bells. We kept running, and I didn't look back. I didn't dare. A man forcefully shoved into Cassie's side, trying to get more speed. I stumbled into the hard, cold wall where I felt a sharp pain as my ear scraped the brick.

I almost tripped, dragging her arm down sharply and almost causing both of us to fall. Luckily, I caught myself in time to catch my foot. That could've ended much worse. I glanced to my left, and right next to me was an enormous beast charging through the streets. Even though I knew what I had signed up for, it was still shocking to be five feet away from a wild animal that could crush you.

I could only glimpse at its side, a pattern of bronze and amber splotches. The color wasn't the only thing that threw me off. The size of this bull was bigger than any kind of bull I had ever seen before. I now understood how people got injured doing this almost every year. These bulls had to weigh at least ten times as much as I did, and their bodies were pure muscle. This wasn't your typical rodeo.

I shifted back into focus after the bulls passed us by. Cassie and I took a quick hurdle in unison over runners who had fallen to the ground. I realized that besides the bulls, the run dangerous because of the fallen runners who could make you trip.

Falling down was the scariest part because once you're down, it's hard to get back up. And if you're really unlucky, a bull might accidentally stumble over you. You see, the bulls didn't *want* to hurt you. They were completely out of their element. They were just trying to run through thousands of human beings to escape the chaos.

As we kept running, the cheering from the balconies and side streets started to become louder. It felt like we were running a race and were getting closer to the finish line.

I could see the bend in front of us, and I knew it was the last turn before the arena doors. We were getting close. I heard the starting pistol go off for the second time, and my mind went to two places. First, the race was halfway over because the first six bulls had entered the arena. Secondly, the second set of bulls had entered the streets. As I processed this, I tightened my grip on Cassie's hand.

The run wasn't over yet. We kept pushing forward and I felt like I was swimming against a strong current. We steered around the bend, and straight ahead I could see the doors to the arena. It was like the light at the end of the tunnel, the peace after the chaos.

In this split second of bliss, a contradicting thought entered my head. I knew the second set of bulls weren't far behind us. The arena seemed so close yet so far away. Momentarily after the thought entered my brain, I heard a man behind me cry out, "*Look out!*" I heard the cow bells and felt the ground tremble once again; then I knew what I had to do.

I pulled us off to the side of the street so I could let the bulls pass us by. I wanted to make it into the arena, but the last thing I wanted to do was get trampled. We were about seventy feet away from the arena doors, and it was going to be a tremendous challenge to make it in on time.

I had my eyes on the prize, though. There was no way I wasn't getting into that arena. I observed the opening, and the doors were much narrower than I expected. Turning my head to look behind me, I felt myself holding my breath.

I watched a ginormous chocolate colored bull charge full speed ahead in my direction. Around its neck hung a collar with a cowbell. It swayed back and forth like a mesmerizing clock that could put you into a trance. Before getting too distracted, I studied the bulls steady gallop. I noticed how it seemed like its body was riding a very low teeter-totter.

I looked into the bulls deep and dark eyes as it passed us by. At that moment, I felt more alive than I ever had in my entire existence. I was fearless, I was courageous, I was brave, and I could accomplish anything. I was invincible.

We would make it into the arena. The five other bulls followed the first, and I knew it was go time. We had about ten seconds to make it. Cassie and I started to push our way through the crowd of people, using as much force as we had to get to those doors.

The last bull entered the arena, and I saw policemen start to close the gates. My pace quickened, and my adrenaline spiked. We were closing in on the gates, and there were seconds left to make it in time. We used our intertwined hands to push ahead, sprinting as fast as we could.

With the worst timing possible, the girl in front of me fell hard onto the ground. She shielded her face from getting trampled. My adrenaline-filled veins made my reaction time quick. I leapt over her like a gazelle, pulling Cassie into the arena. We made it.

MINDFULNESS

"The present moment is filled with joy and happiness. If you are attentive, you will see it." —Thich Nhat Hanh

"When your world moves too fast and you lose yourself in the chaos, introduce yourself to each color of the sunset. Reacquaint yourself with the earth beneath your feet. Thank the air that surrounds you with every breath you take. Find yourself in the appreciation of life." —Christy Ann Martine

Deciding to make the leap to study abroad is one of the hardest parts. The openness and bravery that's required will follow and assist you for the rest of your life. If you've decided to study abroad, there are plenty of skills you gain moving forward. First, arriving at your destination requires observation.

When I arrived in Spain, my curiosity spiked. I was curious the second I entered the airport in Madrid because things were *different*. We become accustomed to the way that we live in our own culture; we accept it as the norm. When our norm becomes our reality, we stop paying attention to the details of everyday life.

To make the most out of life experiences, it's very important to pay attention to your surroundings. The ability to be mindful means being present in one's environment and allowing yourself to feel your emotions. Being mindful can help you make comparisons and observe differences. Mindfulness is important to make the most out of your everyday life.

Before I left, I heard that Spaniards' idea of "on time" meant thirty minutes to an hour later than the scheduled time. My first encounter with this was when I got off the airplane. I waited for my study abroad program director to meet me for transportation to our hotel. I was still surprised and super impatient when they finally appeared over an hour later.

Although my impatience got the best of me, I was mindful that the notion of time varied from culture to culture. Later on, I learned that Spaniards' notion of time was more relaxed. They often took longer eating out at restaurants and spending time with their loved ones. Over time, I realized that just because their idea of time was different, that didn't mean it was better or worse. It just was.

Once I boarded the bus to our hotel in Madrid, I started to notice the little things. Things that never entered my mind before I left. As we drove past speed limit signs, I was in shock.

The white diamond shaped road sign had the number 100 painted across it. The speed limit was WAY too high. *Do they drive abnormally fast here?* I ignorantly asked myself. *Click.* I felt my mind work out the dilemma.

Spain used the metric system, not the imperial system. I later found out that the United States is one of the three countries in the WORLD that doesn't use the metric system. Talk about a wake-up call, huh? Not only that, but they use Celsius instead of Fahrenheit to calculate temperature.

I remember walking into a quaint bar on a street corner with a couple of my girlfriends, looking to pass the time. It turned out, the bartender didn't speak any English. Practicing our Spanish, we engaged in small talk with him as we drank our Estrella Galicia beers.

Of course, our small talk wandered to the weather. It was June, but it felt more like September. It was cold, windy, and frequently raining. It was unusual for that time of year in Spain, so our conversation drifted to how abnormal it was.

I made a comment that in my hometown, the temperature had reached 100 degrees that day! I was still unaware at that time that they use Celsius for temperature instead of Fahrenheit. The bartender looked at me with a cocked eyebrow for a second and then threw his head back, laughing. He then asked me if I lived in a volcano!

It took my brain a couple seconds to make the connection. Before I could explain myself, he had already walked away. I felt a little ignorant, but it was definitely a learning opportunity. I was finally becoming mindful that different cultures live in different ways.

The reason I was noticing the differences is because I was being present in the moment. When you observe the details around you, you learn more about yourself. When you're present, the world seems to get bigger. If I hadn't been present during my experience of Running with the Bulls, I might've never felt the ground tremble. I might've not heard the cowbells or looked straight into the dark eyes of a bull.

Being present also helps you enjoy the simple things. My study abroad group consisted of twelve girls, yet I was the only one who didn't buy a phone plan during our stay.

I know what you're thinking… dangerous, right? What would happen in emergencies? I still had access to WiFi where it was available, and I was always surrounded by my peers who had data. I'm not here to talk about the risks, though. I'm here to talk about the benefits I enjoyed by not having my cell phone while everybody else did.

I remember a specific trip my group took on a bus to the beautiful northern city of La Coruña, Spain. I sat in the back of the bus and could see everyone in my group in front of me. Most of my peers had their headphones in and were listening to music. The rest were trying to sleep.

I didn't have data to listen to music and I wasn't tired. My mind was wandering with curiosity. There was nothing to do other than observe my surroundings. I gazed out of the bus window for the entire trip, admiring the beauty that was right in front of us.

I saw beautiful grassy mountains with wildflowers springing from the fertile soil. Sunshine yellow, magenta purple, and ruby red flowers decorated the verdant grass. The bus swayed through the mountains, and with every mile, the view seemed to get more beautiful.

I thought to myself, how could I be the only one entranced by this beauty? It made me wonder… if I had data, would I have my headphones in too? The two-hour bus ride felt like thirty minutes to me. I had captured a landscape in my memory that I would keep to myself forever. When we finally arrived, my group started to wake up and remove their headphones.

Not having data not only encouraged me to be present it also helped me become better with directions. When my friends and I would plan to go somewhere new in the city, they typically would use their GPS on their phones for directions. Since I didn't have that option, I started to become familiar with which streets led where.

While some of my peers relied on their phones, I used my memory to guide us through the city. Without having data or GPS, I learned how to use a handheld map while traveling. I also started creating landmarks in my brain as clues to help me remember where to go.

Before I left for Spain, I was terrible with directions. It got so bad, my friends back home would sometimes call me "directionally challenged." I was always asking my friends for their addresses to plug into my GPS. I couldn't remember the directions, even after driving there many times.

It drove some of my friends crazy, so I felt pleased to go home with the solution to my problem. All I had to do was be mindful of my environment and not rely on my phone to get around. I finally figured it out.

I experienced Spain without data, and it helped me become more mindful and present. You can still do this, even if you have a phone plan. Going somewhere new and exciting *invites* you to be mindful of your surroundings. Sometimes, being mindful is unavoidable.

The Royal Palace in Madrid is where the royal family occasionally stays. It's strictly prohibited to take any pictures or videos. You're forced to look at the beautiful architecture through your eyes instead of a camera lens. Usually, you can't help being aware of your senses. In the beginning, I felt taken aback by the strong scent of flowers that followed me while I passed them by.

At times, mindfulness is a given. However, practicing this skill can benefit you for the rest of your life. Mindfulness demands attention to details, which can strengthen your memory recall. Observing the world through your senses can give you potential insight.

I gained mindfulness abroad and wanted to practice it in my everyday life. I'm now more present and notice things I never had before, especially directions to my best friend's house. Mindfulness is a skill that anyone can practice. You understand its importance by immersing yourself in a different culture.

ADAPTABILITY

"A wise man adapts himself to circumstances as water shapes itself to the vessel that contains it." —Anonymous

"Intelligence is the ability to adapt to change." —Stephen Hawking

"Don't adapt to the energy in the room. Influence the energy in the room." —Unknown

Those who decide to study abroad learn the key skill of adapting to their surroundings. Soon after arriving at your destination abroad, reality kicks in. Then, your brain switches into survival mode. To thrive in a different setting than you're used to, it's important to adjust to the culture around you. From an evolutionary standpoint, those who adapt survive.

When you learn how to adapt to the changes that life throws at you, you become more resilient. If you're always avoiding change, then change will never come easy to you. You can't prevent change; you can only decide how you react to change.

For instance, in the beginning of my run with the bulls, I was observing the behaviors of others. I waited to start running when everyone else did. This is the initial period when you arrive abroad. Observe the actions and behavior of others. Then, when people around me started to run, Cassie and I followed along, at an awkward pace.

It took a second for us to realize we were running faster than the people around us. We adjusted our pace to a fast jog and finally matched the pace of the other runners. It took a little bit to adjust our pace, but we succeeded through observation and adaptation. Adjusting to a new culture is never easy at first, but everything will fall into place.

I had to adapt to plenty of things to abroad, but first, I had to learn how to greet Spaniards. When I first stepped off the bus in Salamanca to meet my host dad Jorge, he pulled me into a hug and kissed me on the cheek. As an American, I'm used to a nonpersonal handshake with plenty of distance between me and the other person. I wasn't used to this type of introduction. So, after he pulled away, my cheeks burst into hot flames and I refused to make eye contact.

It took me a couple of days, but once I knew this was the typical greeting in Spain, it started to feel normal! Change can be uncomfortable. But, once you learn to adapt and accommodate to the situation around you, it can feel like second nature.

No culture is the same. Every culture has different social norms, education, religion, cuisine, and more. Greeting Spaniards was the first thing I had to adapt to but, most certainly, not the hardest. I had the hardest time adjusting to the meal times and restaurant normalities. Like the left-out milk and meat, I felt surprised how different meal times were.

Like Americans, Spaniards eat three meals a day, but the times they eat are very dissimilar. They eat breakfast around seven in the morning. Then, they eat a large lunch around two in the afternoon and a smaller dinner around nine at night.

When I started this routine, my stomach growled at me every day around seven at night. *I'm staaarving*, it would hiss at me. I knew that if I ate early, my body would never adjust to the eating patterns. Like greeting my host dad, it took a few days of being uncomfortable until I could adjust.

The eating times were different, as was the method of grocery shopping. In the United States, it's typical to go grocery shopping every week or two, buying in bulk. We're a society of Costco memberships and Amazon grocery delivery. We're known for buying canned food for storage. Spain, on the other hand, doesn't follow the same rules.

My host dad went grocery shopping every one or two days. He would buy fresh produce and bread to prepare the food for the day. Since the food contains less preservatives, it's necessary to buy food items as you go.

Another thing I had to adjust to abroad was time. Earlier I discussed how Spaniards' idea of being "on time" is different than ours. I understood that their notion of time was different, I just didn't understand why.

I finally understood after going out to eat at a sit-down restaurant. I'm used to going out to eat in the United States and started making comparisons. I'm a server myself, so I had the routine down. The waiter brings you your drinks, then your food, checks up on you a few times, and then brings the tab. We like to get in and out of restaurants as fast as possible with a quick server. In Spain, it wasn't so much about speed; it was more about spending time with the people you were with.

After the waiter brought my friends and I our drinks, he didn't appear for fifteen minutes. Once he served us our food after ordering, we didn't see him again for about an hour. We were well done with our food and were all growing impatient.

Finally, we flagged him down and paid our tabs. I brought it up to my host family later that night. They chuckled as if it was something they had heard from previous students. My host mom Gabriela gave me a soft smile and said, "Going out to eat is a pastime here. We don't go out to eat just for the food. We go out to eat to spend time with family and friends because we consider it a leisure activity."

I felt my jaw drop. How could I have been so blind? I've lived my life in such a fast-paced environment that I felt uncomfortable when I sat down and relaxed. The server wasn't inattentive or bad at his job; he just wanted to give us time and space to enjoy each other's company.

One other thing I had to adjust to besides time and eating habits was tipping, which, in Spain, isn't a common practice. In restaurants, servers get paid on a fixed salary. They don't depend on making their living off of tips like servers do in the United States.

Also, credit cards aren't always accepted. The bill is usually on one tab for the table. So, we have to figure it out for ourselves. Usually, Spaniards like to take turns paying the bill when out to eat with their friends. It isn't frowned upon to tip, but if you do tip, your leftover change is more than enough.

Spain also tends to be a little more on the conservative side, so I had to dress accordingly. Booty shorts or shirts that showed your stomach led to glares from the older generations. I learned this the hard way. They dress a little fancier, leaning more toward business casual. I ended up buying clothes there and felt glad, as I enjoyed their style.

The adjustment that took the most physical strain on my body was the time difference. I was seven hours ahead of my hometown, and it affected me in more ways than one.

On my first day in Spain, after my group ate lunch, most girls went back to our hotel to nap. That was probably the smarter idea, but I and two other girls decided to explore Madrid instead. We found a cute rooftop cafe and hung out until orientation. When we headed back to our hotel for orientation, I had to force myself to keep my eyes open. My head kept bobbing, and my body was screaming at me to sleep.

I was extremely jet lagged, and I became reliant on coffee to survive. Fortunately, it only took a couple of days for my body and my mind to adjust.

The time difference made it difficult to communicate with my friends and family at home. I learned how to plan around my schedule to Facetime them. When I woke up, they were usually going to bed. Adjusting to a different culture can require physical, mental and emotional strength.

Another physical change I had to make was their scheduled "siesta" or nap time after lunch. It's not required, but Spaniards believe it helps with general health. It was a common practice, and I definitely wasn't against it. This was a habit I was more than willing to take on.

The adjustment period can be challenging but is well worth it. You're allowing yourself to live in a completely different way. You experience a different kind of lifestyle from what you're used to. Adaptability is essential not only in different cultures, but in everyday life.

You have to adapt to the challenges in jobs, relationships, and living arrangements. Life is always changing. So, when you're able to adapt to the changes around you, life becomes a little less difficult. It allows you to become flexible in trying situations and encourages you to go with the flow.

Adjusting to a different culture isn't only about social norms and eating habits. It's also about adjusting to the way that the culture *thinks*. This too, is a beautiful thing. Returning home, I learned to be patient while going out to eat. I learned how to refrain from judgment when the meal takes a while to arrive at the table.

Everybody has to adapt to changes in their lives. Adapting to another culture is a great way to challenge yourself. It's the best way to learn how to adapt quickly. If you can adapt living in a country different than your own, everything else seems like a piece of cake!

WISDOM

"Knowledge comes from learning. Wisdom comes from living." —Anthony Douglas Williams

"The most important thing in communication is hearing what isn't said." —Peter Drucker

You gain so much by traveling somewhere new because you learn things about yourself. It gives you insight into how you relate to the world. Learning is inevitable when you travel. You're surrounded by incoming information at all times. We learn through experiences, history, education, and so much more.

Wisdom isn't solely the accumulation of knowledge or learning. It's the ability to use the acquired knowledge and apply it to your everyday life. Wisdom is taking all that you've learned to make sound decisions and judgment every day. It's generally obtained by your experiences, not just the accumulation of facts.

Gaining wisdom is a given if you decide to study abroad. You can obtain new information anytime. What's cooler is that overseas, you can gain wisdom that will benefit you for the rest of your life. Some wisdom you gain abroad includes effective communication skills and language acquisition. You also become wise because you're expanding your worldview!

Communication plays such an important role in our everyday lives. Nothing would function without it. Human beings want to exchange feelings, thoughts, ideas, and emotions with one another. It's how we relate to one another. This is why we created languages thousands of years ago.

Communication is a category with many different fields. Some aspects of communication are verbal, and others are nonverbal. Some nonverbal cues include facial expressions, body language, and hand gestures. Nonverbals can also vary from culture to culture. When you travel abroad, you're exposed to the different ways people communicate. This makes your communication style versatile. It also puts you at an advantage in the workforce and in your social life.

Being able to communicate effectively can help you reach people all over the world. In your career, you may have to work with someone from a different culture. Effective communication is helpful for conflict resolution, negotiation, and obtaining international relations.

Through my study abroad experience, my communication skills grew in multiple areas. First, I became an expert at nonverbals: hand gestures, body language, and facial expressions.

One chilly night, I met some classmates in the beautiful Plaza Mayor. We were all sitting on the cold cobblestone pavement, exchanging conversation. My friend from Germany introduced me to an Italian girl. She had long, dark, wavy black hair. She had perfectly thick eyebrows, defined cheekbones, and dark eyes.

She immediately threw herself at me and embraced me in a bear hug, pulling away with a grin painted across her face. Her presence brought a warm feeling of welcome, and I already loved how friendly she was.

When we started talking, she spoke to me in very broken English because she didn't know much. When she was struggling with finding the right words, I would try to suggest words.

Sometimes, it worked; other times, I was completely off. It didn't matter, though. Even though there was a language barrier, we were still putting in the effort to communicate. When we talked about our family members, she held up her palm. Her fingers stretched apart showing she had a family of five.

Eventually, we were using our hands to point things out and gesture words. I realized that nonverbal communication can be just as important as verbal communication. Our conversation wasn't an easy ride in the park, but she was one of the most vibrant people I've ever met. I felt honored to meet and connect with her that day.

Let's face it. English isn't the only language out there. So, chances are if you're traveling abroad, you'll be around other languages. Language acquisition is another important part of effective communication skills.

Don't be afraid to travel to a place where you don't know the language. It can seem scary, but I promise you, it's not as hard as you would think. English is a universal language, so there will most likely be signage in English to guide you around. There will be at least someone nearby who knows English and can help translate for you.

Even if you study where English is the spoken language, every country has a different dialect. Even in America, our vocabulary and accent differ from the North, South, East, and West. One of my roommates abroad was from England. Even though we both knew English, we had completely different vocabularies.

"Underwear? That's what you guys call knickers?" she would giggle from across the dinner table. I told her I thought knickers was an even weirder word! We laughed at our differences, but we weren't laughing at each other. We were embracing how different dialects can be in different places. It's completely okay to travel to a country where you don't know a lick of their language. The good news is that if you're studying abroad, you most likely will pick up some of that language.

I've been bilingual since my parents enrolled me in a Spanish elementary school when I was six. I could go on and on about the benefits of knowing a second language (or even a little bit of it). I'll sum up the benefits of what I've learned over the years.

Locals respect you when you speak or even attempt to communicate in the language of the country you're in. It also helps build intercultural relationships, and you can meet many more people! Even picking up a couple of keywords can help you out while you're abroad.

One night, my roommate Vicki and I decided to take the bus to the local cinema. We could've picked a movie in English, but we wanted to challenge ourselves and see a movie in Spanish. My Spanish is decent but watching an entire movie in a second language is still challenging to me to this day.

We decided on the movie "Oceans 8," and gave it a shot. I was happy to see the movie had subtitles in case I got lost. Nonetheless, I tried not to fixate too much on them. During the movie, I was a little slow picking up the jokes. Nonetheless, when it was over, I was proud of how I could comprehend the movie in Spanish!

The point is, you don't have to be fluent to thrive in a country with a different language. You will be at an advantage if you, at least, know key words in the host country's language.

Knowing Spanish was essential for me to succeed living with my host family. After I unpacked my suitcase the first night I arrived at my host family's apartment, it was about time for dinner. We all sat around a wooden oval table. About three minutes into my olive oil and pesto pasta, I realized my host family knew little to no English.

Even though I knew Spanish, not being able to rely on my English was hard in the beginning. I had to either describe words or use hand gestures when I didn't know the proper term for something.

After the first couple of days, I felt mentally exhausted. Being surrounded by a different language for your entire day can take a lot of brainpower. By the end of the week, though, speaking Spanish with them became so easy that I started to dream in Spanish.

After a couple of weeks, my host family complimented my Spanish and how well it was improving. I felt immensely proud of myself for pushing through it.

My program placed me into this host family because I had strong Spanish skills, so don't let this example deter you. Many study abroad programs give you the option to choose an apartment or a host family. If you choose a host family, you're placed with a family that fits your needs. They consider your language skills, roommate preference, and more.

The point of this chapter is to show you that studying abroad can grant you wisdom. You'll be able to learn new dialects or a little bit of a different language! This enables you to communicate with more people than you could've when you left!

Through studying abroad, you become wise in who you're and who you want to be. You grow rich in your experiences, and this can open your mind to new ideologies, values, and beliefs.

When you learn more about the world, it can change how you see it as a whole. Your experiences can change your mindset, attitude, and philosophy. Who knows? Maybe you'll consider a different religion. By traveling and studying abroad, you come closer to your authentic self.

My host family and I would always talk about social issues during mealtimes. We talked a lot about the problems going on in our home countries and made comparisons. No country is perfect. When you hear about the challenges a different country endures, it helps you reflect on your own.

For example, my host family and I discussed the prison systems in the U.S. and Spain. Both prison systems have their issues, but on the opposite ends of the spectrum. The United States has a very high prison population. Sentences can be from one year to a life sentence, including the death penalty. In the United States, the issue isn't putting people in prison; it's how to fund the growing prisoner rate.

In Spain, prisons are lenient. The longest sentence a person can face in prison is 40 years. Sentences are usually reduced on good behavior. They don't have the death penalty. Their problem is the exact opposite of ours. Sentence time is short, and the punishment is mild.

Both countries have issues with the prison systems but in completely different ways. The same goes for gun control. It's difficult to get a gun in Spain. You need a valid reason to obtain a firearm such as being stalked or being military or government personnel. The person then has to undergo a psychological exam, and then the court has to approve it.

In the U.S., all we have to do is pass a background check. There's still violence in Spain, but mass shootings don't occur often.

Learning about societal issues in a different country can open your eyes to your own country. You're able to compare social issues and how each country deals with them. You gain insight on the way your country runs. You can learn what works in a society and what doesn't. It can open your eyes to different government types, law enforcement, and so much more.

Hearing about different government policies doesn't mean you'll change who you are completely. It might make you question biases you've had or challenge the way you think about societal issues. Either way, you see the world through a different lens. It can help you look at problems from many different angles. It also can open your mind to different possible societal solutions.

Through our experiences, we become wise. Through trial and error, we learn how to make wiser and smarter choices. Wisdom allows us to be more well-rounded individuals. It allows us to look at many different sides to each story.

To live a life of reason, one has to take the sum of what they learned and apply it to their everyday life. Language acquisition and communication skills don't constitute all the wisdom gained abroad. Nor does an expanded worldview.

You learn responsibility, individuality, proper decision-making skills, and organizational planning. To be wise is to grow rich from experiences then use those experiences to flourish moving forward. Studying abroad is a perfect way to gain wisdom about the world. The more you see of the world, the wiser you become.

SKILL 6

EMPATHY

"Self-absorption in all its forms kills empathy, let alone compassion. When we focus on ourselves, our world contracts as our problems and preoccupations loom large. But when we focus on others, our world expands. Our own problems drift to the periphery of the mind and so seem smaller, and we increase our capacity for connection–or compassionate action." —Daniel Goleman

"For the world to be better, we should choose the pain of empathy over the comfort of apathy." —Michael RX

"Leadership is about empathy. It is about having the ability to relate and to connect with people for the purpose of inspiring and empowering their lives." —Daniel H. Pink

In our lifetimes, we all deal with tragedy. Whether it's a broken heart, a lost loved one, or unfortunate circumstances, we all know and live through pain. Empathy is the ability to understand and relate to the feelings of others.

It's like the metaphor of walking in another person's shoes for a day to understand what they go through. Empathy is important to respond to situations effectively. It's important whether we're consoling someone, cheering them on, or, at best, listening to them.

Empathy allows us to help each other in hard times as well as support each other in good times. It's the foundation for any healthy relationship. It's what essentially connects us all emotionally.

Going abroad is a great way to learn how to empathize. You see firsthand the difficulties a different country faces. Yes, we can sympathize over tragedies that take place around the world. But seeing it with your own eyes is a completely different story.

Studying abroad made me realize how small my problems actually are. I'm stressed about where I'll be living after graduating college or what I'll be doing for my career. So what? Some people don't even have the opportunity to attend college or get to decide what they want to do for their career!

Not only that, but some people don't even have a roof over their heads or enough money to put food in their stomachs. When I left for study abroad, I knew my own difficulties and the things that stressed me out. I tuned into my own emotions, but understanding what other people felt was harder for me.

I admit, my empathy grew when I left my home town. I strengthened this skill in two ways. The first was learning about Spain's 36-year-long dictatorship. The second was seeing the effects it had.

In an economy and society elective I took, we talked a lot about the history of Spain and their government. We discussed other topics, but, for me, the dictatorship of Francisco Franco stuck out the most.

Francisco Franco graduated as a cadet in the Spanish army in 1910. At the age of 33, he became the youngest Army general in Europe. Two years later, he became the director of the General Military Academy in Zaragoza, Spain.

Franco continued increasing his rankings in the military. He eventually ran for government elections. Franco rose to power in 1939 during the Spanish civil war and won the war for Spain. Afterwards, he established the government as a military dictatorship, as a totalitarian state. Franco outlawed all other political parties. This resulted in all other parties merging to the fascist party.

Once he gained control, Franco violated human rights for Spaniards. Franco established over 100 concentration camps during his dictatorship. He exploited prisoners of war, homosexuals, and political dissidents.

Franco forced the people in the concentration camps into doing labor such as mining coal, building highways, digging canals, and other physical labor. Those who Franco saw as "irreversible" were often shot. Many died from malnutrition or starvation.

Before I left for Spain, I had heard of Franco, but I never knew how extreme the circumstances were. Torturing and killing innocent people wasn't the only thing Franco did. He also drove Spain into an economic crisis that still haunts their country today.

After the civil war, Spain was struggling. Their economic resources such as gold and foreign exchange disappeared. The war reduced productivity, which led to reduced product in agriculture and industry. Countries were also reluctant to help out because of Franco's allies. Franco won the war with support from Nazi Germany and the Kingdom of Italy.

For a decade, Spain was in a severe economic depression. Franco adopted a "self-sufficient economy" that was anti-market policies. Inflation rose as well as black markets. Many people lost their jobs and ended up homeless on the streets.

During the cold war, Franco became anti-communist. The United States supported him on this ideology and began to help. The US started to implement military bases in Madrid. In the early 1950's, Franco abandoned his "self-sufficient economy." He delegated economic authority to technocrats. With new economic delegations, the economy started to grow again.

Today Spain has a parliamentary monarchy as their government. Nonetheless, the effects that Franco left have not left their country. Many family members still mourn their lost loved ones from the concentration camps. Some economic problems are still seen today.

The unemployment rate in Spain has been high after Franco, and reached 14.7% in October of 2019. The United States at that time had an unemployment rate of 3.6%. Comparing that to the United States, their unemployment rate is significantly higher. Adults usually had to live with their parents until their late twenties. Rent was too expensive to afford otherwise. Although Franco died, the economy is still suffering from his dictatorship.

Hearing about the tragedy that Spain endured for almost forty years shook me up. It shocked me how I didn't know much about the topic before I left. I decided to attend a museum of the history of Franco's dictatorship and was even more astonished. On the walls hung photos of the concentration camps with a list with names of those who died. It was tragic.

This country had gone through something devastating, and my heart felt for them. However, my host dad placed the importance of empathy in my heart on that trip. The first day I met him, he showed me around the city. We walked on the cobblestone streets, through the sandstone buildings toward the university. On the outskirts of the plaza sat a homeless man with no shoes and a dog with matted fur.

It wasn't new for me to see a homeless person. I had seen a fair share in the United States. The sight wasn't unusual to me, but the reaction of host dad was. As I was steady in my pace to keep walking, I noticed he wasn't by my side anymore. I looked back and saw him opening up his wallet and handing the homeless man 10 euros.

Jorge gave a soft smile and nodded humbly when the man religiously shook his hand, thanking him. The homeless man had a spark in his eye that wasn't there before. It wasn't the action of giving the man money but the look in his eyes that made me realize how impactful empathy can be.

As we walked away, the mood was different. We walked in silence for a few moments. Jorge explained that he understood how it must be hard not having a home, or not knowing the next time you would eat. He lived in a country where unemployment and homelessness weren't unusual. Jorge didn't live through the dictatorship of Franco. Even so, he lived through the economic effects that followed after his death.

I'm forever grateful to have taken that walk with my host dad because his empathy moved me. It has changed my life. It encouraged me to put myself in other people's shoes to understand what they're going through. Now, I don't like to jump to conclusions about anybody. Instead, I spend a minute trying to imagine what it would be like to be them.

I have a close friend who traveled to South Africa, and he felt affected the same way. He empathizes with others because he has seen starvation. He has seen what they do to survive. When you travel, you'll begin to understand that your struggles are one of a thousand. You'll begin to understand why empathy is essential in living in a harmonious world.

I felt empathy again on my trip after the running of the bulls when a bull was released into the arena where runners taunted it. Runners teased and harassed the bull, trying to make it angry. Watching the bull try to defend itself made me sad. The bull had no control over its environment and had no way to escape. I felt it was cruel and unfair.

The more we can relate to the feelings of others, the more we can live in an interconnected world. Empathy isn't limited to feelings of loss or sadness. You can also feel empathy when someone succeeds or feels proud. You're able to support your relationships through empathizing with your loved ones. Empathizing means supporting your loved ones through whatever emotions they're facing.

Empathy leads to mutual understanding and respect for one another. I remember telling Jorge how much I loved Kebabs and was sad to leave them behind before I left to go back home. On the last night I was staying with my host family, I walked into the kitchen ready for my last meal. On the counter were Kebabs from the restaurant from across the street.

Jorge walked into the kitchen and gave me a small smile. It was a simple gesture, but it brought tears to my eyes. I was so thankful. By listening to my glumness of having to leave Kebabs behind, he did something meaningful for me. By using empathetic skills, he showed me how much he actually cared about me. In the beginning, I worried that I would only be another student to them, that they would only see me as one of the many they hosted throughout the year. As the days went on, I understood that they were a kind couple, who deeply cared for each student they hosted. They listened to our needs and treated us like we were their own.

My host family taught me the importance of empathy. Without empathy, nobody would be able to see eye to eye, and conflict would loom over us like a dark cloud. Empathy is necessary to live in a healthy society. Gaining this humanistic skill can help you prosper in relationships in your life. Traveling is a good way to show you how we're all human, connected by our emotions.

GRATITUDE

"In ordinary life, we hardly realize that we receive a great deal more than we give, and that it is only with gratitude that life becomes rich." —Dietrich Bonhoeffer

"The more you praise and celebrate your life, the more there is in life to celebrate." —Oprah Winfrey

Just like everything in life, the journey of studying abroad will come to an end. If you decide to study abroad, you'll gain beneficial lifelong skills and learn so much along the way. The journey is a transformative experience, but you don't stop learning once it's almost over.

When your time is almost up, you gain insight on your trip you didn't have before. You start to reflect and think about all your experiences. When I had one week left abroad, I remember feeling saddened with a heavy heart. I didn't want to leave. I wanted to stay there forever.

But I took that sadness from my heart, and I turned it into gratitude. I was grateful that I had the opportunity to learn so much about the world and grow along the way. Being grateful can help you appreciate the little things in your everyday life. Not only that, but you'll be less likely to take things for granted. Gratitude allows you to cherish the relationships you have and what they bring to you. It also opens the doors for new relationships to unfold.

When you're grateful for what you already have, you forget about the things that you *want*. Life isn't about what you could have, it's about being grateful for the things you already have. If you're always wanting more, how can you be happy with the things that are already yours?

One of my favorite celebrations is the Fourth of July. My family owns a house on the lake, and we live in the perfect location to enjoy all the festivities.

Each year, my family invites friends and relatives over in the morning to walk to the parade. It's perfect because it's only a block away from our house. We usually spend the day out on the lake, swimming, waterskiing, and tubing. When nighttime rolls around, we all gather around the beach in front of my house. We get front row seats to watch the fireworks that are set off on the lake.

The Fourth has always brought me pleasant memories growing up. On that note, I was a little bummed out that I would be missing it while I was studying abroad. It was one of the family traditions I always looked forward to, and one of the few I wouldn't be there for. At the end of June, my study abroad program director informed us there would be a firework show. Fireworks would be set off over the river once it got dark.

I knew I would be missing the fourth, so I decided to go. My friends and I made our way down the street where a crowd gathered to watch the magic happen. I was stuck in a negative mindset, thinking that there was no way it could compare to the Fourth of July that I knew.

My friends and I settled near the back of the crowd, waiting for the show to begin. My eardrums filled with the whine of a firework shooting into the sky. With a loud boom, the sky was lit with vibrant green lights. Another firework exploded before the other vanished. The lively colors blended together in a beautiful mix.

The fireworks were being let off quicker than I had ever seen, and it was magnificent. I never saw different colors blend in the way they had. It was a show of a lifetime. Red and yellow fireworks appeared, symbolizing Spanish pride.

I felt a rush of emotions wash over me, and, all of a sudden, I was crying. I was the opposite of disappointed; I felt amazed. The disappointment of missing out on the Fourth of July at home was replaced with gratitude for something just as special.

It wasn't just the fireworks I was grateful for. Despite the fact, I was content. Good friends, a cheerful crowd and beautiful fireworks surrounded me. I wouldn't have wanted it any other way. I was grateful I had experienced a new kind of Fourth of July and the happiness it brought me. This wasn't the only time I felt gratitude on my trip abroad.

A block away from my host family's house was an enormous park. The park had every kind of flower you could ever imagine. The air always smelled fresh, and my step always felt lighter when I strolled through the park. It was a place that was perfect for everybody: kids, grandparents, teenagers, and adults.

It had an enclosed dog park, a pond to feed the ducks, and a playground for the kids. For the adults, it had an ice cream shop and a plaza where elders danced on Wednesday nights to salsa music. It might sound silly, but when people ask me about my "happy place," my mind doesn't wander to a vacation setting. It doesn't wander to where there are sandy beaches or mountain tops. I think of the sound of birds chirping, a warm breeze, and light gleaming on my skin in a pattern designed by the trees.

The park brought me comfort, relaxation, and gratitude. Almost every day after class, I would walk to the park and process everything I experienced from that day. I would settle down on a blanket under a tree. Sometimes, I would listen to the birds sing, and, other times, I would read.

When I had a week left of class, my feet wandered to my happy place. I laid down my blanket and got comfortable in my usual spot. I lay down, stretched out, and felt the prickly grass on the palms of my hands. Light trickled through the tree branches and I felt the warmth of the sun resting on my face.

This was a place I had grown to love. With only one week left in the astounding Salamanca, I felt a rush of overwhelming emotions take over. Randomly, I began frantically sobbing. I felt my chest rise and fall in abrupt patterns against the ground beneath me. I could hardly catch my breath.

I wasn't surprised that I was crying; my heart adored Spain. What surprised me, though, was the reason behind my tears. I was sad I was leaving, yes, but my tears came from a different place in my heart. I was shedding tears of gratitude.

I was so grateful and felt so blessed to have had the opportunity to travel to an amazing city. I was thankful I got to learn about the world and about myself, and to have found my "happy place." I was grateful for my family and friends for supporting me through it all. I was thankful they made time for Facetimes, despite the 7-hour difference.

I was grateful for the faculty members at my university who helped me get there. I was grateful for my host family who had greeted me with welcoming arms and loved me like one of their own. I was grateful for my friend who dropped everything to visit me for a week.

I was grateful for everyone who pushed me to where I was at that moment. I was grateful for all the lessons I learned, and I was grateful for all the personal growth I experienced. I was grateful for everything that had happened to me in those two months. I appreciated every moment with all of my being. Never again would I let my desires blind me from my blessings.

For me, it took the end of my journey to really appreciate everything that I had experienced. It was a time of magnificent transformation in my life and, for that, I couldn't be more grateful. When life seems unfair or I'm driven by a desire for something I don't have, I remind myself of that moment in the park. It reminds me that there's *always* something to be grateful for, even when it doesn't feel like it.

All in all, my study abroad experience was the most beautiful thing that has ever happened to me. The gratitude I felt will follow me for the rest of my life. Now, I understand how important it is to appreciate the efforts that your friends and family put into you. Every heartbreak or set back is an opportunity to grow, and I'm grateful for the lessons they teach me.

Even though I don't have a Mercedes Benz, I'm okay with my 2003 Honda CRV. My air conditioning doesn't work in the feverish summers in Minnesota, but the heat works like a gem in the winters. Hell, I didn't have air conditioning the entire time I was abroad!

If you're alive and healthy, have people who love you, and have a roof over your head, you have a lot to be thankful for. When I came home, I gave more hugs, made more phone calls, and started thanking people more. Not only does gratitude make you feel good on the inside, it can make others feel good too. You can share your gratitude by letting them know how much you appreciate them.

When you travel, you start to understand how privileged you actually are. You start to understand that the little things you take for granted aren't available in other places. I'm a sucker for Root Beer, but Spain only had Fanta and Coke. When you see the world, you stop taking your simple pleasures for granted.

UPON YOUR RETURN

The Arena

We made it into the arena. We put on the brakes and slowed our sprint. I looked behind me and realized there were only two other people who had made it in right before the gates were closed. We had made it with seconds to spare, and I noted how perfectly everything had played out.

I walked about fifty feet out of a dark tunnel into an open, circular arena with sand at my feet and my soul on my sleeve. The arena seats surrounding me were completely packed. The stadium engaged in a loud uproar. I looked ahead, and saw the bulls disappearing into a tunnel opposite to where we entered.

As soon as I made it into the center of the arena and stopped walking, that's when I felt it. The adrenaline rush I'll never forget. My heart was pounding, and I had a smile painted on my face. The tip of my toes and fingers were delightfully tingling. My whole body felt like it was experiencing a natural high.

I felt powerful and indestructible. At that moment, I forgot about my sprained ankle altogether! In that second in history, I was worry free. The crowd was still going wild, and I knew right then and there, I would carry with me everything about the moment forever. I was a champion, and nobody could ever take that away from me. It was a defining moment in my life.

I've always been a risk taker and someone who loves adrenaline rushes. At that moment, I knew that adrenaline was a drug I had become addicted to. I never wanted to be sober again. I stayed in that state of pure euphoria for a couple minutes. Then, the crowd started to scamper about and draw closer to the edges of the arena.

Cassie and I had made it into the arena, but we had no idea what to expect after that. We exchanged concerned glances, and we followed the crowd. We made our way toward the cement walls that blocked off the spectators. I heard a ticking noise coming from the big flat screen TV off to my right. Once my eyes caught sight of the TV, I felt horrified.

The ticking noise continued as a timer counted down from ten seconds. Out of the corner of my eye I saw about six men lay flat on their bellies in the sand. They laid down like a stack of logs on top of each other in front of the doors the bulls had entered. I was curious about what they were doing. My focus shifted to a ringing buzzing sound as the timer reached zero seconds.

My ears filled with the song "Tubthumping" by Chumbawamba. For those who don't know what song I'm talking about, the chorus goes like this: "I get knocked down, but I get up again, you're never going to keep me down." It was comical, really. Suddenly, doors from the tunnel opened, and out came a copper-colored energetic bull. It started charging toward the men on the ground.

I felt myself holding my breath. I only exhaled once the bull leapt over the stack of men who were braver than even I felt. The bull slowed his pace to a halt in the middle of the arena. It was a short second before men started running toward the bull in attempts to harass it. I finally got it. The song lyrics matched the mood entirely. They couldn't have chosen a more perfect song.

The bull started to charge whenever someone would make sudden movements. Anytime it got anywhere near us, Cassie and I would pin ourselves to the cement wall. Sure, the run was exhilarating, but having a bull run at you instead of next to you is a different kind of rush.

As time went on, people in the arena started to become braver, and got closer to the bull, taunting it. Some people got a little too close and ended up getting head butted by the bull's horns. Some got launched into the air by the bull and were thrown onto the hard sand. It was amusing to watch; however, I would never be one to charge at a wild animal that weighs ten times as much as me.

As much as it was entertainment, I did feel sad for the bull. Cassie and I decided to exit the arena, as the arena became a hectic mess of commotion. It wasn't even nine in the morning, but it felt like I lived a lifetime in that single hour.

We had been learning about the San Fermín festival for a decade, and we had finally experienced it firsthand. Sure, it was scary at first. We had to be open to the idea of getting injured and endured the bravery to take the risk. We had to adjust our pace, be mindful of our surroundings, and learn about their tradition. We also felt grateful that we were in Spain at the right time. We were in Spain; we still had to plan to make it to Pamplona during the festival.

I even felt empathy for the bull. It might've only been an hour in my life, but I learned so much in such a short time. Pamplona became a special place in my heart, reflecting back on that day. I had entered Pamplona nervous and not knowing what to expect, but I left Pamplona without fear.

I started the run that day as a comfortable calf living in the meadows eating grass. I ended the race that day as a bold bull, taking on the world horns first. That run gave me the ability to understand myself better. It gave me the ability to overcome obstacles (literally and figuratively). And lastly, it gave me the bravery to get in the race and not just be a spectator on the sidelines of life.

AUTHENTICITY

"Unlike a drop of water which loses its identity when it joins the ocean, man does not lose his being in the society in which he lives. Man's life is independent. He is born not for the development of the society alone, but for the development of his self." —B. R. Ambedkar

"When things change inside you, things change around you." —Unknown

A huge take away of my study abroad experience was getting to know myself better. Visiting a country with different values encourages you to do some inner reflection. Reflection is a great way to understand yourself better. You'll be able to note your strengths and the areas you could improve on.

When you reflect back on your experiences, you're able to focus on the emotions that you felt. Understanding your inner feelings strengthens emotional intelligence. Becoming in-tune with your emotions makes it easier to respond to emotional stimuli. You can respond to emotional stimuli rather than reacting to it.

Through reflection, you boost your emotional intelligence. You can identify your core values through inner reflection as well. Once you clearly identify your core values, you can act accordingly. Using integrity, you can make decisions reflecting your values. The good thing is, you can be the one to decide which values you wish to have.

Some inner reflection is necessary to become a better version of yourself. You can figure out the gap between who you are, and who you want to be. Through self-reflection, you gain self-awareness and a clearer image of your identity.

Everybody has weaknesses. That's what makes us human. What's important is how we look at our weaknesses. If we look at our shortcomings as part of our personalities, we might feel that we're unable to change them.

We're individuals who are consistently changing with the flow of everyday life. I'm not the same person I was yesterday. I still know I have areas in my life I need to work on. Our weaknesses do not define us, but we always have room in our lives to become better people. Nobody's perfect, and nobody expects you to be.

It's important to know your own shortcomings so you can act accordingly. Instead of blaming yourself for your weaknesses, you can see them as something to improve on. Self-improvement can lead to humility and maturity.

One thing that I noticed abroad, was that Spaniards strongly value their relationships. Around two in the afternoon, most, if not all, businesses close for their lunch break and stay closed for a couple hours so that people can eat lunch with their families.

When I found out, I felt stunned, but it made me respect their culture even more.

Coming from the United States, consumerism is highly valued. I have to admit, it was kind of refreshing they valued relationships over profit. Not only do they value their family, they make sure to make time for every connection they have.

Even though I was only one student, my host family made me feel like I was part of their family. Not only did we eat every meal together, we spent at least twenty minutes afterwards, talking. My host family took time out of their days to get to know each one of their host students. They always made sure we felt at home.

One night, in attempts to get to know Vicki and me better, my host mom Gabriela suggested that all three of us have a cooking night. She suggested we make a dish from our home town. Before dinner, we all strolled to the supermarket with our lists of ingredients. It was nice to spend quality time, the three of us. It's one of my favorite memories abroad.

I decided I wanted to make American tacos. Vicki decided to make roasted rosemary potatoes and a fancy dessert. I figured that tacos were an easy meal to make, and surprisingly my host family had never tried them before. We scanned each aisle as we walked through the grocery store. I grabbed beef, lettuce, tomato, and onion from the produce aisle. Gabriela helped pick out the best tasting products for the best prices.

The one thing I had a difficult time finding was sour cream. I tried to explain it to Gabriela as best as I could and google translate wasn't helping me either. We stood in front of the dairy refrigerator for what felt like ten minutes. I was trying to figure out if the store carried sour cream. Finally, I grabbed a container, hoping it would be the right stuff. I was hoping it wasn't a coffee creamer.

We hauled our grocery bags back to the apartment and settled around the kitchen table. Vicki started to play Spanish music, and the fun began. We shuffled around the kitchen, rotating between the cutting board and the stove. We danced to the music and enjoyed each other's company.

I was so comfortable, I felt like I was cooking in my own house! The one struggle was helping Vicki figure out baking measurements for her dessert. The directions pulled up on her phone were in English, but we were using Spanish measuring cups. The abbreviations for tablespoons, teaspoons, and cup sizes were completely different letters. It was a learning experience in itself.

The potatoes came out of the oven right as I finished slicing the veggies and cooking the beef. Everything was ready to consume. We all gathered around the table to eat. We then put the dessert in the oven to bake. I was very eager to see what they thought about American tacos.

Gabriela complimented us on our cooking skills. She gave a satisfied smile when biting into the taco, and I felt proud. I made everyone two tacos each, and about half way through the second, she declared she was content and full. We waited a few minutes before taking out the dessert and digging in.

It was an amazing bonding experience. It made me feel appreciated because she wanted to get to know us better. We aren't her immediate family, but she still treated us with respect. She gave us her time and showed an interest in our backgrounds. Spaniards enjoy making connections and spending quality time with their loved ones. I admired it so much that I decided to make it one of my core values.

Traveling through Spain, I could see their values of community in their architecture. In each major city, the center would consist of a square shaped plaza. Stores, restaurants, ice cream shops and tourist information surrounded each plaza. Tables and chairs would line the outer walls for a place for people to sit and enjoy meals together.

Oftentimes, live events would take place in the center of the plaza for everyone to enjoy. In Salamanca, they had an orchestra concert, salsa dancing, and guitar playing. One weekend, people crowded the entire plaza in Salamanca. People sat and waited for an amazing light show to begin.

The light show is a festival that takes place every year. Displayed on the plaza wall are short video clips of fantastic animation. Each video clip was different. Some showed exuberant patterns and others told a story. The animations only last about a minute each. These video clips come from all around the world, and each has a different song in the background. A variety of music genres was played, but most played techno music.

Everyone in the crowd wore light sticks as headbands or around their wrists. It was magical, seeing everybody enjoy something so beautiful. It definitely gave off a community vibe.

I felt whole and interrelated in each plaza, and it made me feel less alone. Plazas are places for the community to gather to enjoy each other's company. They served as a way for people to be a part of something greater. I've always valued my independence. Something changed, though. I was starting to understand the importance of community.

I don't have a huge family, by any means, but we definitely don't get together every day for lunch. If I'm lucky, I get to see them more on the holidays.

Coming home, I did a lot of introspection on how active I was as a family member. I realized that I wasn't pleased with my efforts in staying connected with my family. Sure, I was away at school, but that didn't mean I couldn't visit them more often or call more.

I decided that I wanted to make family as one of my top priorities. Even if I have to put my cell phone down during dinner, I wanted to strengthen my family connections. I still have plenty of room to grow; however, identifying what I want to improve on was the first step.

When I came home, I prioritized family as one of my core values by self-reflection. Looking back on who I am helped me understand some of my imperfections. First, I needed to put family first more often. Secondly, I needed to slow down.

One of the trickiest things for me when I arrived in Spain was learning how to relax and be patient. Like the example I used earlier about dining out at restaurants, I figured out I was a very impatient person.

In the United States, we live in a fast-paced environment where we want to see results quickly. One of my biggest weaknesses is impatience. Even though I'm aware, my study abroad experience emphasized this problem. Things take time, and patience was a virtue I was willing to practice.

I also understood that I had independent tendencies. At first, I didn't see this as something I needed to change. Yet, I knew I wanted a balance between my independence and maintaining my connections. I'm a very stubborn person, so it's difficult for me to ask for help sometimes.

I can't do everything on my own, and it's okay to ask for help. People actually enjoy helping others out. I knew I had to swallow my pride and ask for help when I needed it in the future.

Through self-reflection, I understood myself a little bit better. I was able to identify things that I wanted to improve on.

Coming back, I prioritized family as one of my core values. I decided to work on being more patient. I also decided to start asking for help when I needed it.

Self-reflection doesn't necessarily mean that you need to change who you are or what you believe in. It simply means that you're interested in becoming self-aware. Looking at the world through a different lens encouraged me to reflect on who I was. It encouraged me to work toward the person I want to be.

Through reflection, we can understand our identities and improve our emotional intelligence. We can decide to make healthy decisions that will guide us toward our core values. When we know the character traits we want to possess, we have the ability to act accordingly.

Different cultures hold different sets of values. Immersing yourself into a different culture helps you better understand what you value. It's the perfect opportunity for self-reflection. I knew I wanted to be a better me coming home. It was in my hands to bring that person back to the United States.

RESILIENCE

"Resilience is accepting your new reality, even if it's less good than the one you had before. You can fight it, you can do nothing but scream about what you've lost, or you can accept that and try to put together something that's good." —Elizabeth Edwards

"When we are no longer able to change a situation, we are challenged to change ourselves." —Unknown

Coming home from studying abroad can feel similar to entering the arena. You're processing everything from your trip and shock is still flowing through your veins. However, once the shock wears off and you get back into your daily routine, you may have an overload of emotions to process.

You enter another adjustment period coming home. Unlike adapting to a new culture, you're adjusting back to the culture you left. Adjusting back is about applying the new you to your old lifestyle.

For me, adjusting back home was the most painful part of the entire experience. I learned so much and made such fond memories; I didn't want to return to my old life. Sure, I missed my friends, family, and my own bed, but I felt more alive abroad.

I never felt as *myself* as much as I did abroad. I could be whoever I wanted to be. It turned out, I just wanted to be a better me. Going through times of transition is painful, but it only makes us stronger individuals.

I had been home for a week before returning to my college town, Duluth. I was on my way to reunite with my friends after spending the summer apart. It was the last weekend of summer break, and I felt both nervous and excited to see everyone again. I felt anxious butterflies in my stomach as I reached the Duluth exit.

Once I got to my friend's house, I took a deep breath, grabbed my belongings, and headed inside.

As soon as I walked through the front door, I saw my close friends sitting on the living room couches. "Sam! You're back!" one of my girlfriends exclaimed, jumping up from the couch, extending her arms for a hug. "Hi!" I announced, a grin painted across my face.

It felt great to see everybody again, but I felt taken off guard by her statement. "You're back!" I replayed it back in my head. It's a simple statement, really. A fact, if you will. It was genuine and sweet and a gesture saying she was excited I was home. But as I embraced her in a tight hug, I felt confused about how I felt, being back.

The weekend seemed to fly by as the weekends usually do. The weekend was filled with socializing and catching up. Everybody was sharing their summer stories, reminiscing. I was happy to see all my beautiful friends again. They had become family since my freshman year. I had never felt as accepted for who I was from a group than I had from them.

Still, I felt off. I packed up my things Sunday morning to head back home. I still needed to pack before the semester started. As soon as I slammed the passenger door shut and fell into my seat, I felt tears trickle down my face. I was emotionally and mentally drained.

My boyfriend at the time saw I was crying and asked what was wrong. That only made me cry harder. Tears flooded out of my eyes, and, in a choked voice, I responded, "I don't feel like I belong here anymore." He grabbed my hand and attempted to comfort me, but never in my life had I felt so alone.

I felt like my friends knew the old me, the person who I was before I left. The new me felt like a stranger who stuck out like a sore thumb. I had changed so much while I was abroad. I was so flustered and overwhelmed, fearing that nobody would accept the new me.

It felt like I had lived a lifetime abroad and all I wanted to do was share it with the world. Don't get me wrong, my friends asked how my trip went. I just had so much to say yet wouldn't know where to start.

The conversations felt surface level, without any meaning or depth. They never seemed to last longer than five minutes. It really made me frustrated. Yet, it wasn't their fault. They wanted to know every detail about my trip. I just didn't know how to put my words into meaningful dialogue, and I felt misunderstood.

After experiencing something so life changing, Spain was all I wanted to talk about. It was all I ever thought about and talked about for months afterwards. In casual conversations, I would always make cultural comparisons or share a memory.

I wanted philosophical conversations. I was thinking about the world in a different way. I felt like nobody really understood the mental shift I had experienced, no matter how much I wanted them to. I was around people whom I loved and people who loved me back, yet I felt all alone.

Eventually, my sadness turned into frustration, and I was angry at the world. I felt so misunderstood like nobody cared to hear how my experience changed me for the better. Of course, my friends cared; they're amazing people who have my best interests in mind. They just hadn't experienced what I had. That, in itself, made it difficult for me to relate to those around me.

After all, my mindset had changed, and I didn't think the same way anymore. I had different ideologies and values and had gained valuable experiences. I had a strong desire to see more of the world.

I talked about Spain so much that I felt like I annoyed others by it. For six months after I returned home, I missed Spain so much, I could feel my heart ache. I felt a mixture of sadness and anger when things would remind me of Spain. I avoided looking through my pictures abroad at all costs.

A couple of times, tears would fill my eyes walking past study abroad posters in the hallways. The poster of Spain had pictures of Salamanca's plaza mayor. All I wanted to do was go back.

I felt out of place, like I wasn't meant to be living in Minnesota anymore. The only place my mind would wander was Spain and the time I had spent there. It was dreadful.

Even though I returned home, I was still learning from my trip. I saw things I didn't see before about the American culture. I noticed differences in education, teaching, and our social lives.

I compared eating and exercise habits, law enforcement, and countless other things.

My trip gave me so much to think about, and since I felt misunderstood, in time, I became quiet. It caused problems in my relationship because I was always in my head. I couldn't communicate my thoughts to him, and he felt there was distance growing between us. Little did he know, he was the only person I thought could understand what I was going through.

He had studied abroad about six months before I did, so he knew where I was coming from. One day we were sitting in the car, listening to music and he softly noted, "You've been in your head a lot lately, and I never know what you're thinking." He looked down at his hands while he spoke.

I sat there not knowing what to say because I was oblivious that my silence was obvious to other people. He continued, "I know that you have a lot going through your head. I know I did when I came home. And I know you're probably missing Spain because I know I still do."

For once, I felt heard without having to say anything at all. A tear trickled down my cheek and off my chin. For the first time in months, I didn't feel as alone.

Those first couple of months home were the hardest for me. I fell into a reverse culture shock depression. It had me questioning where I belonged in this world. Nothing seemed to make sense anymore. I knew it was going to be difficult leaving Spain because I had left a piece of my heart there. A piece that would stay there forever.

Adjusting to home was the hardest thing I've gone through in my entire life. But the pain eased, and I found my place again. That miserable and unbearable pain I felt turned me into a warrior. I built up resilience through the pain. Now, it's easier for me to adjust to major life changes.

It taught me how to be strong and to be grateful for the things that brought me to where I am today. One year after my trip abroad, I moved back home from college after graduating. Going from living on your own back to life with your parents can be a big adjustment. At least it was for me.

Nonetheless, my experience of returning from Spain made it easier to adjust afterwards. I found it easier to recover and I felt like I had thicker skin. Maybe adjusting back home won't be the hardest part of your experience. Maybe it will be adjustment to the culture or homesickness.

Either way, studying abroad is a beautiful and messy experience that isn't always easy. Nothing good in life comes easy. The hard times are what make you strong and resilient for the rest of your life. All the beauty was worth all the pain.

LEADERSHIP

"The function of leadership is to produce more leaders, not more followers." —Ralph Nader

"Leaders become great not because of their power but because of their ability to empower others." —John Maxwell

If you decide to study abroad, all the skills you'll gain will manifest into one great character trait. You become a leader. You learn how to stand up for what you believe in. You find your voice. In a world full of followers, a leader is one of the best things you can be.

Building leadership skills can benefit you throughout your entire life. It will benefit you whether it's in education, a hobby, your career, or relationships. You can inspire initiative as a leader and make the change you want to see in the world.

Coming home, I felt like I couldn't relate to others, and it made me feel voiceless. I felt discouraged and hopeless. Have you ever felt like you had an amazing idea you wanted to share but couldn't properly get your message across? That's how I felt returning home.

After about two months, I knew I didn't want to wallow in my self-pity any longer. I decided to turn my pain into something good. I was sick of feeling unheard. So, I put myself in a position where I would be heard by the people who needed to hear it the most.

One day, I charged into my study abroad office not knowing what I was looking for. All I knew was that I would be able to relate to the people in the office who had studied abroad, too. It was almost like I was a stray dog looking for a pack.

I strutted in and took a seat on the closest bench. I didn't know what my next move would be. At least it felt nice getting away from the busy hallways. Voices traveled like buzzing bees, and it was nice being in the quiet. I took a big sigh, feeling stupid. I was about to stand up after a couple minutes of sitting there to make my way to my next class. That's when the study abroad program director walked in.

He helped me with my study abroad application, so it wasn't the first time we had met. "Sam!" he greeted, smiling and walking closer. "How was your trip? How does it feel to be back?" he asked, genuinely curious. I bit my lip, screaming on the inside at my emerging tears to go away.

There was that phrase again. Being "back." "It's been okay," I said looking down at my hands. "I miss Spain and it's the only thing I can think about," my voice wobbled. He gave a half smile, standing directly in front of me now. "Well, you aren't alone in that. Come into my office," he ushered, "I have something you might be interested in."

Two months later, I stood in front of a classroom of thirty of my peers. Public speaking had always made me nervous, but I knew I had to get my voice out there. I felt all eyes stare at my every movement. I passed around business cards addressed to the study abroad office. Once everyone had a card, I clicked my computer screen and began.

"Hi everyone. My name is Sam, and I studied abroad in Salamanca, Spain for two months this past summer." I clicked through a slideshow of my pictures, highlighting the memories I made and what I learned. I finished my presentation then passed out information on study abroad sessions, how to get started, and who to contact.

Overall, my speech was only scheduled to take five minutes. When I looked at the clock, ten minutes had passed. I had gone over, and I realized I wasn't even nervous anymore.

It didn't even feel like public speaking, because I was talking about what I was passionate about. The presentation was over, and the class applauded. I was already looking forward to my next presentation.

This internship helped me get through the difficulties adjusting back. I felt rewarded when people asked questions or came up to me in the hallways asking for more information. I felt as if I were planting a seed to encourage people to take the leap abroad.

My internship required five classroom presentations and ten hours of volunteering. I blew through my classroom presentations, enjoying them.

For some of my volunteer hours, I decided to take part in an informational table. I didn't study abroad through my university. I studied abroad through an affiliate program, Academic Programs International. API was tabling that day, so I was stationed there.

It was the last hour that I needed to complete my internship. I was a little bummed out that it was ending. I knew either way that the opportunity alone had helped me feel better about coming home. Without seizing the opportunity, I would've most likely still been wallowing in self-pity.

Once I reached the API table, I swung my backpack off my shoulders. I glanced up to see a young woman with short, blonde hair, extending her hand. I went to shake it. "Hi!" she enthused. "I'm Hannah, the director of Alumni engagement for API. Where did you study abroad?" I was overjoyed by genuine curiosity. I told her about my trip and how life-changing it felt. She asked me where in Spain I traveled to, what my favorite food was, and how I liked my host family.

Finally, I thought to myself. She was asking all the right questions. Between talking to students, we shared stories from our study abroad experiences. Toward the end of my tabling shift, she had informed me of an internship through API. The internship was called "Global Leadership Academy." I was immediately intrigued. On my way to my next class, I pulled out my cell phone and typed it into my search engine.

Winter break approached, and my internship through my university was over. I wasn't done speaking out about studying abroad, though. I was far from it. I had already submitted my application for the Global Leadership program. All I was waiting for were my letters of recommendation.

To be quite honest, I applied to the program within a couple days of speaking to Hannah. A couple weeks passed, and I uploaded my letters of recommendation. Soon after, I got an email congratulating me on my acceptance to the program! I was ecstatic. In a couple months, I went from feeling voiceless to becoming the voice for study abroad. I had a voice, I just had to find the right audience.

Spring semester started, and I went back to information tables and classroom visits. The difference was that for API's internship, I also got to plan events around my community! I decided to organize a Spanish painting night with "tapas." A "tapa" in Spain is like an appetizer in the U.S.

It was a learning experience, planning an event all on your own. I had to book a room, market the event, and order appetizers from the universities catering team. I actually had to send them recipes and figure out the billing information that they would send to API.

Responsibility doesn't feel like a chore when you're doing it for something you're excited about. I was nervous that I wouldn't get too high of an attendance rate. But I put up flyers, and the study abroad office helped me market my event. I felt excited when I had about twenty people show up!

I spent the night talking to other students who had either studied abroad or wanted to study abroad. We shared delicious food and painted watercolor onto canvases. Of course, a handful of my best friends showed up to support me and keep me company, too. I was so proud of myself for being vulnerable enough to fail but brave enough to try.

Summer was drawing near, and I felt proud of myself for putting myself out there. I created a voice within myself. I was advocating for what I believed in. I was bringing people together and building a community around me. I had so much fun promoting studying abroad that it didn't even feel like work to me.

As an incentive, API offered a $600 travel voucher to students who were creative with their event planning. I was so impressed by the events that my peers were planning, I wasn't expecting to receive the voucher. The internship was over for a month and I received an email in my inbox from API. In the email, API congratulated me on receiving the $600 travel voucher.

I was stunned, but I had never felt so proud of how far I had come. I started the year off feeling alone, depressed and voiceless. But by putting myself out there and becoming a proponent for the things I believed in, I had never felt so fulfilled.

As spring semester ended, I received my degree and moved back home. I was grateful that I had found the opportunities for such amazing internships when I did. Still, I was curious what I would do next. For six months, I worked, paid off loans, and applied to graduate school. Then, something exciting happened. Hannah reached out to me once again.

I wasn't too surprised, because I had reached out to her two months earlier for a letter of recommendation. I scanned the email and my mood changed completely. I reread the email paying closer attention and let out an excited squeal. She had included information on another internship opportunity that started in January.

Hannah wrote: "Hi Sam! I wanted to pass along this campus relations representative position for the spring. It's basically an internship that would allow you to travel and represent API for a few months this spring. I thought it might be of interest to you, since you applied for grad school in the fall. Let me know if you have any questions or want any additional information. Thanks so much, Hannah."

At the time I received this email, I was feeling like I was living on autopilot. Wake up, go to work, go to bed, repeat. My life was stagnant, and I knew I had to start doing something I was passionate about again.

I felt ecstatic to hear about the fantastic opportunity. I also felt flattered Hannah had reached out to me about the position. Even a year after I had studied abroad, I was still seizing opportunities to continue to talk about it.

Today, I'm sitting at the airport in Chicago writing this book. I'm waiting for my flight to board to head back home to Minnesota. This was my first week as a campus relations representative through API. I traveled to three different campuses in Wisconsin and Illinois. I visited classrooms and hosted informational tables.

I encouraged a handful of students to sign up to learn more information about study abroad. I was doing what I loved, but also gaining real-life experiences. I was becoming a leader.

I had booked my own flights, hotels, and drove my first rental car. It's only my first week, but I've already learned so much. I've learned how to manage a budget, plan efficiently, and create professional connections.

I'll spend the next three months traveling throughout the Midwest. I'll travel to Minnesota, Wisconsin, North and South Dakota, Kansas, and Nebraska. I'm excited to inspire students to step out of their comfort zone and into the world that awaits them.

My study abroad experience had turned me into a leader. I want to encourage others to become leaders, too. The world should be explored and adored, and it always has room for more mentors. I have developed a goal of higher study abroad participation rates.

Anybody can have a voice if you address your speech to the right audience. Leadership can benefit you in your personal and work life. It improves productivity and encourages others to do good work.

Leadership grants you the opportunity to make connections. It leads to new directions in life and opens doors. My recovery process would've taken much longer if I hadn't decided to visit my study abroad office. I never would have met Hannah or had the opportunity to work for API.

I built a professional relationship with Hannah. Building that connection led me to another internship opportunity through API. If I had never become a leader, I wouldn't have made the crucial connections I had. If I hadn't put myself out there, I would've never found those amazing opportunities.

It's up to you to seek out and pursue opportunities that support the life you want to live. One door always leads to another. Do you want to lead, or do you want to follow? It's easy to follow the pack, but it takes a courageous spirit to lead it. Anybody can become a leader with dedication, inspiration, and compassion. If you decide to make the leap, I promise that you too can change the world.

CONCLUSION

Looking back at my experience abroad, I never would've imagined that I would be where I am today. I was a completely different person a year and a half ago than who I am now.

My openness and bravery led me to an experience that completely transformed who I am. It provided me with skills I never knew I needed and opportunities I never knew existed. Along the way, I gained wisdom. I learned how to apply the skills I learned into my everyday life. I learned how to be mindful, empathetic, grateful, and adaptable. Returning home, I was more authentic, more resilient, and I became a leader. I had amazing experiences, gained beneficial connections, and became curious about the world.

You experience a whole range of emotions studying abroad but in the best way possible. It can be challenging, overwhelming, and euphoric all at the same time. Going abroad, I wish I would have had a resource to guide me through all the emotions. It would have been helpful to know it was okay to feel the way I felt.

This was one of my intentions for writing this book. Coming home, I felt all alone. If I can combat that feeling of loneliness for one person, I'll feel satisfied. I'll admit, it was also very therapeutic to write.

Another intention I had for writing this book was to encourage more students to study abroad. In a diversified world, it's important we learn to treat each other with compassion. We need to respect and empathize with one another. Human nature breeds difference, and conflict is inevitable in the world. That's why it's so important to learn how to understand one another.

We shouldn't let our differences divide us, we should allow our differences to unite us. If we shift into that mode of thinking, the world becomes a place of love and unity. It's not in our best interest to judge others for having different perspectives. Instead, we should embrace different ways of looking at things.

Studying abroad benefits an individual for the rest of their lives. They become more well-rounded, more authentic, and more understanding. Studying abroad demands the practice of valuable life skills. It leads to incredible opportunities in your education, career, and social life. It also allows you to reflect on who you are and work toward the person you want to be.

I believe that we create the life that we manifest. Would you rather let fear be the driver of your life, or would you rather be behind the wheel? Would you rather hide from the changes life throws at you, or would you rather seize the change? Would you rather take charge and be a runner in the race of life, or just be an observer who watches it pass by?

Would you rather live wishing for the things that you don't have, or live cherishing all the things you do have? Would you rather follow or lead the pack?

It all falls into your hands. Are you living a life that leads to exponential growth? It's up to you to seize every day to become the best version of yourself. Improve not only for yourself but also for those around you.

Now, ask yourself, "Am I ready to take the leap abroad?"

NEXT STEPS

If you're thinking about studying abroad after reading this book, here is what you can do to get started:

1. Start researching. Brainstorm locations that interest you, and then pick out your top three locations.

2. Consider your options. Think about if you want to go to a big city or a small town. What language do you want to study? Do you want to live in a dorm, apartment, or with a host family abroad? How long do you want to go for?

3. Meet with your advisor. Discuss courses you need in order to graduate. Look into cost of programs, scholarship and fellowship options available, and how you can budget your money beforehand.

4. Apply. Look into admission requirements, deadlines, and documents required for the application.

5. Start researching the host country. What are the social norms? What about cultural differences? What kind of food is typical in that country?

For more information on how to apply to study abroad, download the free workbook from the link in the beginning of the book. In the work book, you can work through these considerations while taking notes. The work book also provides checklists, information on what to pack, a budgeting page, and things to research before you leave.

ACKNOWLEDGEMENTS

I'd first like to say thank you to my Dad. I aspire to be like you in every single way. I wouldn't have written this book without your encouragement. If I hadn't joined my dad on The Best Year Ever 2019 Blueprint in San Diego, I wouldn't be here today.

I'd like to thank Chandler Bolt for creating Self-Publishing School. You made my dream of writing a book seem tangible and realistic. Thank you to the mastermind community for being so supportive and uplifting.

I couldn't have written this book without my excellent coach Gary Williams. Gary always had the perfect advice and encouraged me to push through my fears and mental blocks. Thank you to my Editor, Wayne Purdin, for being timely and efficient. Thank you for your helpful suggestions and making my ideas clear. Thank you to everybody who helped me with my cover design, formatting, and market my book. Thank you to all of my launch team members, as well as everyone who gave me their input during the process of publishing.

I'd also like to thank Hannah Olevson who has pushed me and believed in me since day one. You truly are a leader who inspired me to become one, too. I thank Hannah and the API staff for their guidance. API provided me with opportunities that inspired me to become a leader.

Thank you to everyone involved with my study abroad experience. Thank you to my resident director, Miguel Blanco. My study abroad experience wouldn't have been as amazing if it hadn't been for you. My biggest thanks go out to my host family. Since the first night, you made me feel special and important. You always treated me with respect and taught me so much about the world and myself.

Thank you, Cassie, for chasing adventures with me for my whole life. You have always encouraged my bravery. Hand in hand we have taken life by the horns. Our bond is forever, no matter life's circumstances or the physical distance between us. I know you'll always be by my side through the ups and downs that life has to offer.

Thank you, Barry, for being my rock when I felt lost and uninspired. You never doubted my ability and always cheered for my accomplishments. Thank you. Savannah Dettman, Tayler Erickson, Savannah Buck, and Lucas Bohmert. You all have supported me along the way. Thank you to all my other close friends. I hold you close to my heart for always listening, giving advice, and cheering me on.

Thank you, Mom, for always having faith in me and letting me know you're proud. Thank you to the rest of my family. Every single one of you is amazing.

Self-Publishing
School

NOW IT'S YOUR TURN

**Discover the EXACT 3-step blueprint you need to become
a bestselling author in as little as 3 months.**

Self-Publishing School helped me, and now I want them to help
you with this FREE resource to begin outlining your book!
Even if you're busy, bad at writing, or don't know where to start,
you CAN write a bestseller and build your best life.

With tools and experience across a variety of niches and
professions, Self-Publishing School is the only resource
you need to take your book to the finish line!

DON'T WAIT

Say "YES" to becoming a bestseller:
https://self-publishingschool.com/friend/

Follow the steps on the page to get a FREE resource to get started
on your book and unlock a discount to get started with Self-
Publishing School

ABOUT THE AUTHOR

S amantha Kaiser is a 21-year-old graduate from University of Minnesota, Duluth where she earned her Bachelor's of Arts in Communication and Hispanic Studies. Her parents enrolled her in a Spanish immersion program at the age of 6. Since then, she has practiced her bilingualism for 15 years in many ways. She practiced and practices through education, traveling, volunteering, internships, and studying abroad.

Samantha was an intern for her university's study abroad office. She participated in Academic Programs International's global leadership academy. Samantha travels around the Midwest as a Campus Relations Representative. Every week, she advocates for opportunities abroad. Although traveling is her #1 passion, cuddling up to her dog with some Chinese food and a good movie comes in a close second.

CAN YOU HELP?

Thank You For Reading My Book!

I really appreciate all of your feedback, and
I love hearing what you have to say.

I need your input to make the next version of
this book and my future books better.

Please leave me an honest review on Amazon letting
me know what you thought of the book.

Thanks so much!

Samantha Kaiser

Printed in Great Britain
by Amazon